1

2

3

4

5

6

7

8

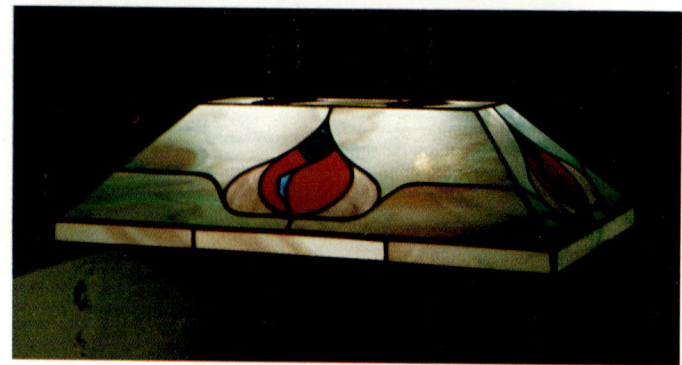

9

10

11

12

13

14

15

16

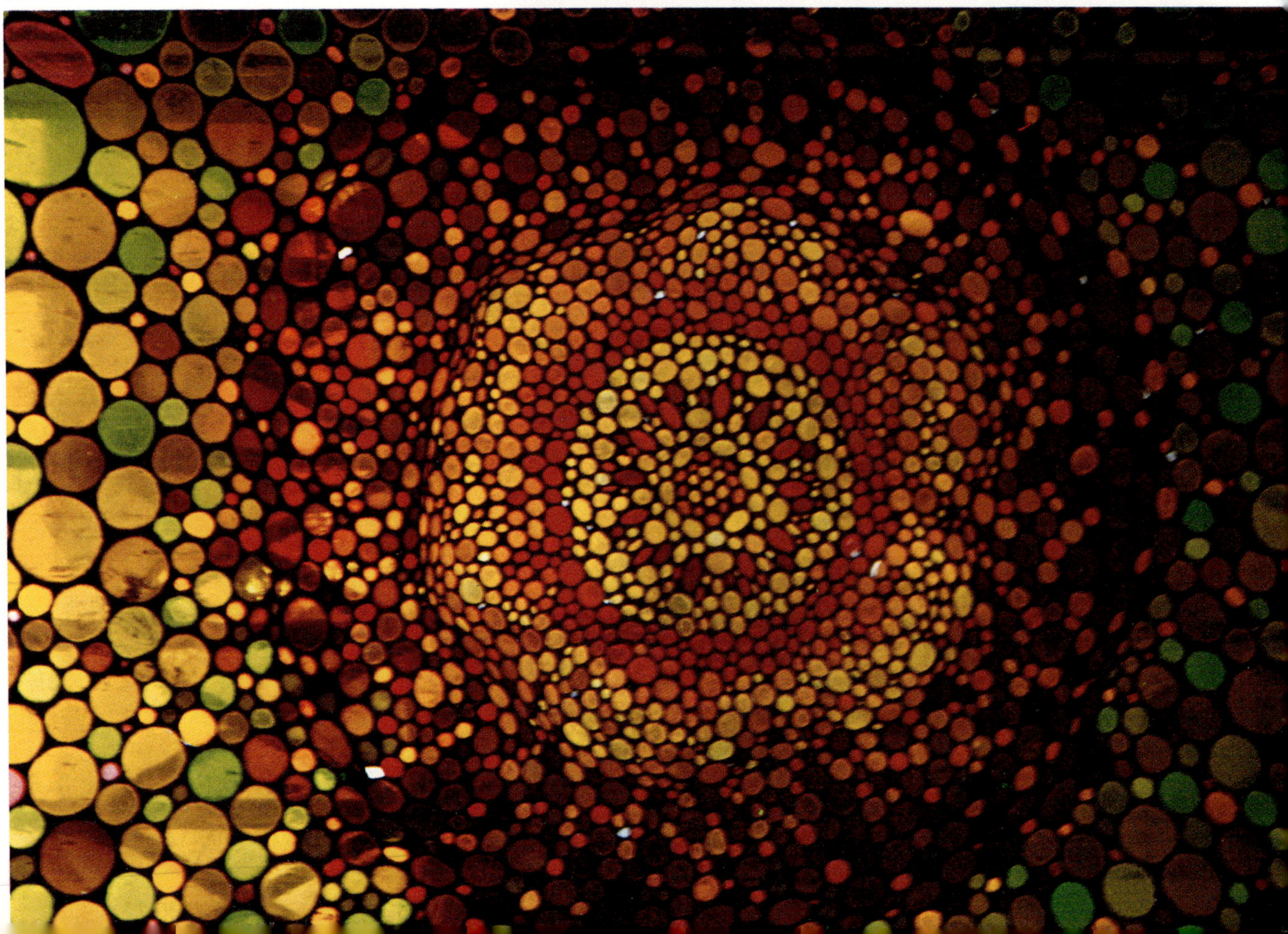

21

22

GLASS-WORKS
THE COPPER FOIL TECHNIQUE OF STAINED GLASS

JENNIE FRENCH

VAN NOSTRAND REINHOLD COMPANY
New York Cincinnati London Toronto Melbourne

Van Nostrand Reinhold Company Regional Offices:
New York Cincinnati Chicago Millbrae Dallas
Van Nostrand Reinhold Company International Offices:
London Toronto Melbourne

Copyright © 1974 by Litton Educational Publishing, Inc.
Library of Congress Catalog Card Number 74-12748
ISBN 0-442-22442-7 (cloth)
ISBN 0-442-22443-5 (paper)

All rights reserved. No part of this work covered by the copyright hereon may be reproduced or used in any form or by any means—graphic, electronic, or mechanical, including photocopying, recording, taping, or information storage and retrieval systems—without written permission of the publisher. Manufactured in the United States of America.

Designed by Rosa Delia Vasquez

Published by Van Nostrand Reinhold Company
A Division of Litton Educational Publishing, Inc.
450 West 33rd Street, New York, N.Y. 10001
16 15 14 13 12 11 10 9 8 7 6 5 4 3 2 1

Library of Congress Cataloging in Publication Data

French, Jennie, 1947-
  Glass-works.

  1. Glass craft. I. Title.
TT298.F73   748.5   74-12748
ISBN 0-442-22442-7
ISBN 0-442-22443-5 (pbk.)

Credits and Acknowledgments

Creations in glass pictured in the book are by: Larry Brooks, Jewel Bishop, Jaropolk R. Cigash/Family Guild, Gilly, Ori Halber/Light Industries, Lori Sanchez, Leandro Valasco, and the author. Photographs are by: defrancis/soundandfuryfilm Ltd., Leonard Mastri, Elbrun Revere, Constance J. Russell, William Sears, and the author. Line drawings are by the author, except for the first, which is by H. Russell-French.

I would like especially to thank Laura Kiaulenas, who taught me to draw; Larry Brooks, who taught me stained glass; Gail Aiken, who typed the manuscript; all the photographers and glassworkers who gave their time quite freely, especially Peter DeFrancis; Michael Drons, who edited the manuscript; and my mother, without whom this book would never have been.

Color Pages

C-1. Stained glass at S. A. Bendheim Company in New York City. At top, Bendheim's third floor, with its thousands of sheets of imported antique glass and its huge, sliding sample racks. At center and lower left, some imported antique-glass samples. At right, the street level at Bendheim's, where domestic and rolled glass are stored and displayed. If you work with glass, you know about Bendheim's; they literally supply almost everyone in America with stained glass—even Tiffany was a regular customer in his day. (Photographs by defrancis.)

C-2. The studio and glass creations of Ori Halber. At top left, a workbench and a lamp. The pliers are cut-running pliers that have specially curved jaws for breaking glass. At top right, a detail of a lamp that is basically the same design as the lamp at top left, except that it lacks the bottom skirt. Notice the excellent soldering work. At center right, another lamp photographed from above. At bottom right, a second workbench and another lamp. On the bench are a soldering iron, a roll of copperfoil, templates, metal shears, and a metal cutting guide. At bottom right, a lamp cut from domestic rolled glass that requires multiple lighting fixtures for proper light distribution. A little over a year ago, Ori used a rough draft of this book and another book on the lead-came method to teach himself stained glassworking. He often uses very large pieces of glass, but his craft level is so high that his lamps are solid without needing additional reinforcing. (Photographs by Sears.)

C-3. Three views of a lamp by Jaropolk R. Cigash. At top, the full lamp, cut from domestic rolled glass. At left, an aerial view; at right, an interior detail. Notice the narrow beading. Jerry chose to minimize the look of the lead bead in this lamp. By doing so, he weakened the lamp's structure, which he compensated for by adding reinforcement in the form of copper wire soldered into the interior joints and base perimeter of the lamp. His work is so good that the reinforcing is invisible and the fragile-looking lamp is solid. (Photographs by Revere.)

C-4. The unusual lamps of Gilly. This artist has used everything but sheet glass for these lamps—traffic-light covers, glass doorknobs, jewels, prisms, mirrors, even bottles. At top right, an interior detail of the lamp at top left. (Photographs by defrancis.)

C-5. Gilly's large window mural, measuring ten feet in diameter. At bottom, a detail of the mural, slightly flattened by the camera's lens. Gilly began the mural on the floor with a single piece of glass no larger than a nickel. With the help of a few friends, a keg of beer, and tons of popcorn, he raised it to the window. The surrounding wall was shaped to repeat the undulations of the mural. In both lamps and murals, Gilly seems to work without plan or format and makes the almost impossible appear effortless. He does not break rules, but he creates new ones—his own. (Photographs by defrancis.)

C-6, C-7, and C-8. The stained-glass lamps of Leandro Valasco. This artist's approach to glassworking is so unusual that it merits representation in this book even though he works in lead came—the alternate method to copperfoil. His beautiful lamps defy the usual problems of mass production. Without sacrificing craft or design, Valasco manages to sell his lamps for about half the cost of other mass-produced lamps. He includes antique and industrial glass (most commercial lamps use only rolled glass), uses multiple lighting fixtures rather than the single bulb commonly found in store lamps, and he creates unusual round and oval shades. (Photographs by defrancis.)

CONTENTS

PREFACE	14
Chapter 1:	
COLOR	15
Color and Emotion	15
Color Rules	16
Chapter 2:	
GLASS	19
Antique Method	19
Rolled Method	20
Handling and Storing Glass	20
Chapter 3:	
TOOLS AND MATERIALS	21
Cutting Equipment	22
Wrapping Equipment	22
Soldering Equipment	23
Chapter 4:	
THE STUDIO	24
The Studio as a Controlled Environment	24
Portable Studio	26
Safety	26
Studio Furniture	26
Shop Yoga	28
Chapter 5:	
APPLIED DESIGN	30
Some Impossible Cuts and Their Solutions	36
Chapter 6:	
MANUAL	38
Cutting	38
Breaking	41
Grozing and Wrapping	45
Soldering	50
Cleaning and Tinning the Soldering Iron	58
Chapter 7:	
FIRST WORKS	60
Chapter 8:	
SPECIAL PROBLEMS	68
The Curve	68
Freehand Curves	68
Cutting Guides	68
Templates	71
Chapter 9:	
LAMP CONSTRUCTION	73
Preliminary Work	73
Soldering	75
Assembly	79
Light Bulbs	82
Glass Densities	82
Chapter 10:	
DESIGNING ORIGINAL LAMPS	84
Part One: Working Drawings	86
Part Two: Construction Drawings	92
Assembly	96
BUYING GUIDE	102
Retail Companies	102
Small-Quantity	103
Bulk Mail-Order Suppliers	103
Shipping Information	103

PREFACE

Back in 1968 I learned stained glass, ran a studio with two friends in New York, and enjoyed my craft while making a few dollars. Soon after we dissolved the studio in 1970, I began toying with the idea of writing this book. Since then I have had a few more studios and taught several people the copperfoil method of stained glass. Believe me, it is a lot easier to teach someone in person than to write it all down in a monologue. A lot of give-and-take discussion and demonstration gets lost in the translation.

If you came to me to learn my craft, we could talk about glass for a long while, and then I could demonstrate how simple it is to cut and break glass. I would have you cut your first piece on our first meeting together—taking care to choose a large piece of beautiful antique glass that I knew would excite you visually and surprise and delight you when it broke as easily as a cracker. Once you have cut your first piece, half of your fears are gone, and you can immediately begin to think of glass in terms of its intrinsic possibilities.

Unfortunately, this cannot be. Let me at least try to answer some of your first questions. The question I am most often asked by my students is what is the difference between this copperfoil technique and the method used for church windows—and which is better? Church windows and many commercial lamps use sections of grooved lead came to hold the pieces of glass together. The only soldering needed with lead came is at its joints. This is a very functional way of joining glass—most suitable for architectural and mass-production work. Lead came, however, is flat and uninteresting in itself. At twenty feet overhead in a stained-glass window, it is fine. My concern in that instance is with the color and design of the glass—not with the aesthetic value of the joining medium.

But at eye level it's a different story. With lamps, window panels, and boxes, your eye immediately notices how the glass is joined. Here, I feel, lead came fails; it is dull. Were it not for its effectiveness in terms of mass production, not even the greediest businessman would prefer it to the copperfoil technique. With this latter method—the method I use—glass is surrounded by an almost fluid lead line. Far from detracting from the glass, this line has a great deal of beauty in itself. And, in fact, the very manipulation and control of this line often becomes one of the greatest pleasures of the technique.

My students' second-most-often-asked question is a bit more subtle. It concerns design. Usually with their first drawing, they ask, "Why can't I do this design in glass?" My eloquent answer often is, "Just because." Glass is just not all that flexible. You must first learn its limits and then set your mind and talents against these limits. I still find myself designing things that I can't cut, like the hourglass shape. I know that as I am making the last break that I'll probably lose it at its thinnest point—but I try it anyway. Wide to thin to wide—it's always trouble and I always try. That's part of it—trying. Later in the book, I discuss such problems and some possible solutions.

I have put into this book what I feel is immediately important for learning how to work with glass—not just the basics but a lot of fine points. But I have excluded some matters. I recommend a couple of ways of breaking glass while holding it with both hands. But I make no mention (except here) of breaking glass off the edge of a table or a workbench. I've done this because I honestly feel that you learn more about glass by holding it in your hands. Another moot point concerns soldering three-dimensional objects. In this book I recommend constructing forms to hold the object as you solder. And yet I often don't use forms myself. If I solder the outside joint of a lamp while holding it in my lap, I am fully prepared to receive a stunning solder burn if a drip rolls onto my leg. Forms all but eliminate this possibility, so I felt I should recommend the safe way only.

Enough of this preface. Turn the page and I will do my best to teach you what I have spent many happy years learning—the copperfoil technique of stained glass. And—please have fun with it.

Chapter 1:

COLOR

Color and Emotion

Light, magician of illusion, passes through glass—touching, expanding, filling, transforming space—and uses color to create and control what it illuminates.

Ill. 1-1

Pen and ink sketch of Chartres Cathedral in France by H. Russell-French.

In spite of the electric light, our instinctive reactions to color, in terms of day/night, remain primitively intact. Day means increased activity (*Homo sapiens,* the hunter), and night means decreased activity (*Homo sapiens,* the hunted, huddled in his darkened cave). It has also been substantiated that our heartbeat, pulse, and respiratory rates are dramatically affected by colors, speeding up for pure red, for example, and slowing down for blue. For centuries, color has been used to guide and control thinking—from the mundane to the magnificent. Small wonder, then, the quiet and profound nature of the temple interior with its rich but muted stained-glass colors—it was planned that way.

What we are dealing with is not so much decoration, but the creation of an emotional environment through the interplay of glass and living light. For a moment, imagine a wooded area during the height of summer, and its moods—in terms of color—as the lighting changes:
just before sunrise when white clouds of
steam rise up from marshes and moist
ground like great ghost fingers against
a purple-blue sky. . .
sunrise-diamonds and rainbows of dew,
covering everything with bright wetness. . .
high noon, drained and exhausted by
its own enveloping heat and moisture
—everything dies for an hour. . .
toward sunset, relief brought by
slanting rays of sun, deepening and
subduing colors while the lengthening
shadows make dark shapes appear and
disappear in the corners of the eye. . .
sunset throws a great celebration
for color, while a hushed forest silently
prepares for things that not only
gobumpinthenight, but glow, flash, and
illuminate as well.

You already have an emotional awareness that belongs solely to you and your experiences—think about your reactions to situations and locate these colors and forms. You might begin with simple unpretentious ideas, but, if the mystery of glass catches you, the translucent walls of your imagination will fill large windows. (The same Louis Comfort Tiffany who inspired the exquisite stained-glass Tiffany lamps also produced a twenty-seven-ton drop curtain containing nearly one million pieces of glass for the National Theater in Mexico City.)

Color Rules

More than two centuries ago, an English physicist by the name of Isaac Newton astounded the world with his discovery that pure "white" sunlight actually contained every color seen by man. He proved his point with two simple prisms. The first spread sunlight into a full-colored spectrum; the second converged all the colors back to white light. There was no doubt that the colors were in the light, and not in the prisms. Like many great discoveries, Sir Isaac's met with a good deal of skepticism and even more righteous indignation—a lot of it from artists. You see, for hundreds of years anyone who worked with pigments, dyes, stained glass, or any colored material knew that white was the absence of color. Mixing every color on a palette produced black—not white.

Newton went further and claimed that the primary colors—from which all others could be derived—were red, blue, and green. Indeed, these three colors dominated the spectrum produced from his prism. Artists knew, however, that *their* three primary colors were blue, red, and yellow. No possible combination of Newton's three primaries could produce yellow—and they could prove it. . . .

This is not the place for a long scientific and philosophical discussion of who was—and is—right. For our purposes, suffice it to say that both schools are right. Color rules based on light conflict with color rules of pigment. Newton could take a beam of red light from his spectrum and overlap it with a beam of green, and he produced yellow. An artist can take red pigment and mix it with green, and he gets a very dark brown. The simple answer is that colors are indeed in light. Take the reddest apple into a dark closet, and it has no color. But the colors in light when reflected and absorbed by a surface (paints, glass, etc.) conform to what we know as pigment rules.

Since stained glass follows the rules of pigments, it is these rules that concern us here. Our entire range of color basically consists of three colors that enjoy a simple relationship to each other. Understanding these relationships is vital to using them when doing stained glass.

The three colors are:
RED BLUE YELLOW
and they combine to make:
RED + BLUE = PURPLE
BLUE + YELLOW = GREEN
YELLOW + RED = ORANGE

As these colors combine in various proportions, they pass through all their different hues:
RED, reddish-purple;
PURPLE, purplish-blue;
BLUE, bluish-green;
GREEN, greenish-yellow;
YELLOW, yellowish-orange;
ORANGE, orangish-red.

Furthermore, every color has an opposite color, called its COMPLEMENT:
RED—GREEN
BLUE—ORANGE
YELLOW—PURPLE
When complements are added together, they make different hues of brown:
RED + GREEN = very dark BROWN
BLUE + ORANGE = medium dark BROWN
YELLOW + PURPLE = dark BROWN

To clarify these rules for yourself, hold a piece of red glass over a piece of blue glass and examine the resulting purple; then combine a blue with a yellow. Next place a red over a green and obtain dark brown.

Ill. 1-2

Color rules of pigments.

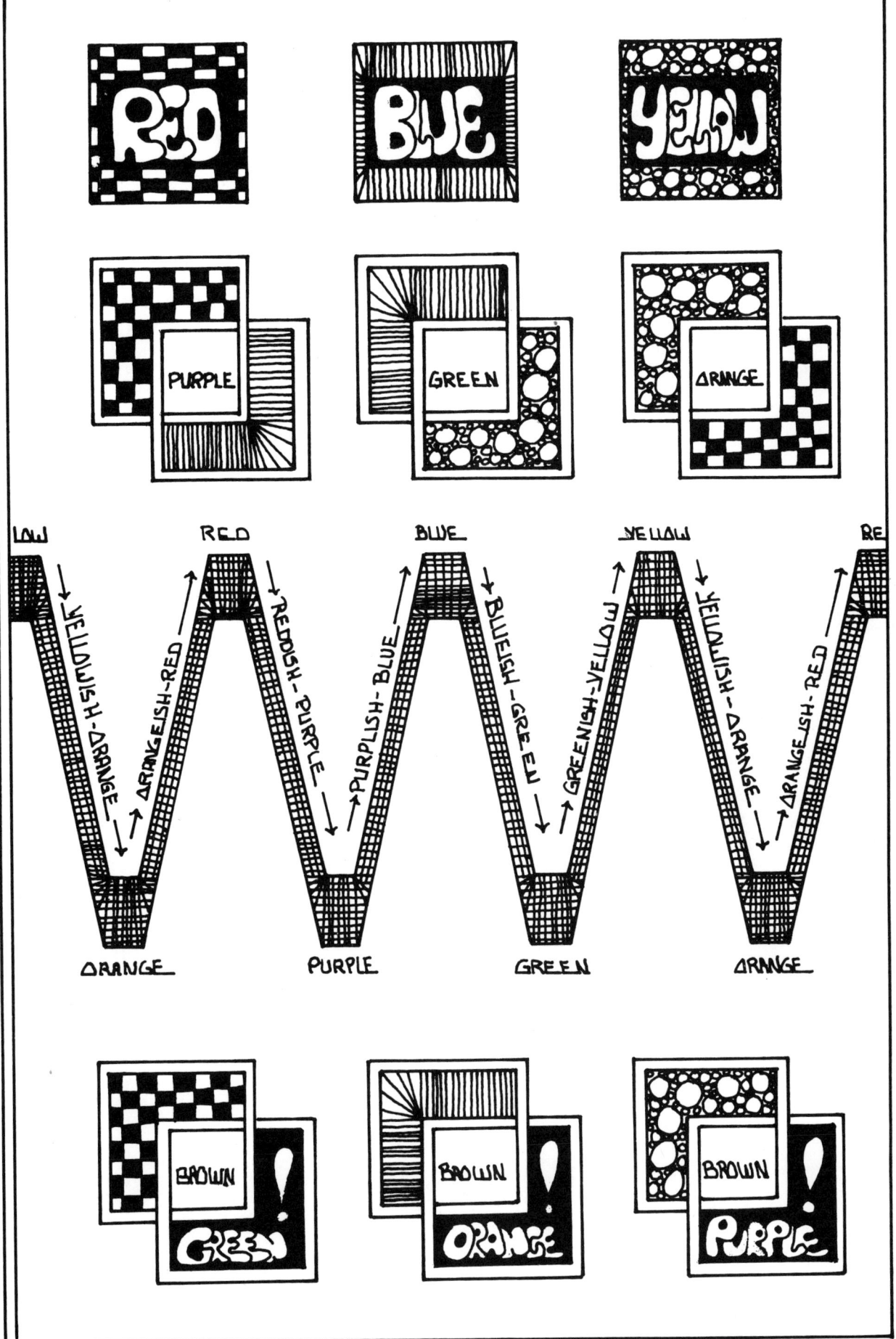

All other colors are derived through an increase or decrease of lightness, darkness, and intensity. Using references to paints, the three ways of color change are:

(1) Adding WHITE makes all colors pastels (tints); adding BLACK subdues or mutes all colors (shades);

(2) an increase of YELLOW lightens or brightens ORANGE, GREEN, and BROWN, while an increase of RED or BLUE darkens or deepens all colors except YELLOW;

(3) adding turpentine (transparent glass) thins or lightens, while adding linseed oil (opaque glass) thickens or makes cloudy colors.

Pigment rules are merely a method of isolating and interpreting natural phenomena; they contain little magic or confusion on their own. What is more important and exciting than any rule is locating your own responses to color, light, and form. To do this, start from scratch; throw out taboos and prejudices.

A fast way to learn something really new about yourself is to experiment with those colors you have previously rejected. If you detest green, make a panel of different green glasses—antique, opalescents, etc.—then study the results. Try the off-colors (that netherworld of weird tints and shades)—or, if the idea of noncolor sounds foolish to you, defiantly make a panel of five different textured, clear glasses.

Glass is intrinsically beautiful, and it is only through extraordinary effort that you can make it less so.

Chapter 2:

GLASS

Before you buy glass, you should understand most of the descriptive selling names; otherwise (despite the fact that nearly all sheet glass is suitable for copperfoil work), you might buy a domestic rolled glass when your project actually would have profited much more from an antique glass. Sheet glass is designated for either art or commercial (industrial) purposes and is either domestic (made in the U.S.A.) or imported (made in France, Germany, England, or elsewhere).

Within the art-glass category there are two manufacturing methods—the antique method (so called for its ancient origin) and the rolled method. These two methods of manufacture produce an awesome range of glasses from which to choose, with differences within differences. The first parts of both methods are similar: sand, soda, ash, and metal oxides are mixed together and heated to a molten state (about 2500° F.). After this, however, the methods and results begin to differ radically.

Antique Method

A gob of molten glass is picked up on the end of a blowpipe and blown and turned until it forms a large, hollow shape, like a long, glass balloon. The bottom end of this glass balloon is cut off, and then the end still attached to the blowpipe is removed. This leaves a standing cylinder open at both ends, approximately three feet long with a twelve-inch diameter. The cylinder is then cut lengthwise, turned on its side, and placed in a reheating oven, where it opens, flowerlike, to become a flat sheet of glass. At this point, the hot sheet of glass (now about 1000° F.) must be cooled to room temperature in an annealing machine. This gradual and even heat reduction removes brittleness and reduces stress within the glass.

Antique glass, which can be either a domestic or an imported glass, is noted for its beautiful imperfections called reams, bubbles, or striations. Its method of manufacture—blowing—limits the size of a sheet to less than half of a rolled sheet. Below are the main types of antique glasses:

Solid comes either clear or in colors. Because there are literally thousands of available colors, it's possible to locate forty different hues of one basic color. Imported antique glass is especially brilliant, transparent, and easy to cut.

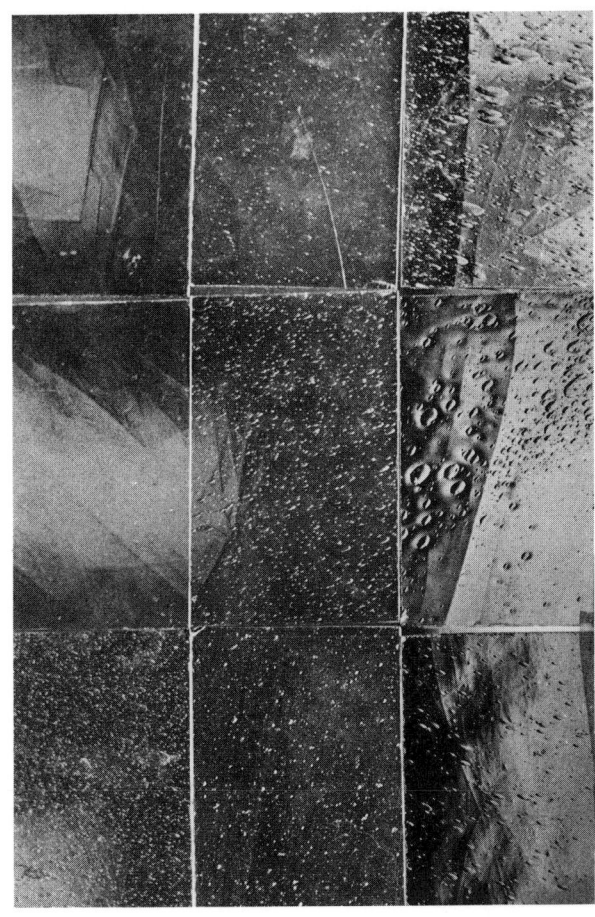

Ill. 2-1

Samples of solid, antique glass, both clear and colored.

Streaky is an almost overdramatic glass—with swirls and streaks of either different colors or one basic color that moves in on itself, plus all the desirable imperfections. This glass is highly transparent, sometimes overpowering, and always difficult to cut.

Reamy is a relative of streaky, but it does not change in color but rather in texture. It is easier to cut.

Flash glass has two layers: one a thick, base color and the other a thin, flash color. The two layers may be different colors, for example, white flashed with red (an opaque glass used for etching), or the same colors; deep reds, blues, and greens are very often flashed. Flash glass is always cut on the thick, base side.

Rolled Method

Molten glass is gathered up in a large ladle and poured into a rolling machine. The machine then rolls out a sheet of hot glass onto a metal cooling plate. In this method, as well as the antique method, the slow-cooling process is virtually the same. Rolled glass is usually a domestic glass of standard, uniform thickness. It is available in a very wide range of colors and patterns:

Cathedral (domestic sheet): This glass is made in more than 100 colors and many pressed patterns—granite, Flemish, smooth, double rolled, hammered, moss, mottled, etc. Some kinds are also misnamed. For example, seedy antique is actually seedy rolled. Each pattern cuts differently and affects light in its own specific way. The colors are generally solid and slightly murky.

Opalescent: This is a semi-iridescent glass that is most often smooth on one side and granite-backed (pebbled) on the other. It is a glass of many colors, combined in great washes and splotches. These opalescents are most like the original Tiffany glass and emit a rich glow when lit from behind. Opalescents are fairly easy to cut and break.

Opal: This semiopaque glass is usually smooth on both sides and generally found in milky, marbleized colors. It gives a warm, diffused glow when lit from behind.

These are the basic kinds of sheet glass found in a well-stocked supply house. Choose your glass not only for color and pattern (texture) but also for density. Glass will be transparent, translucent, semiopaque, or opaque. In terms of light and design, these varieties produce a movement from brilliant, clear glass to muted, glowing glass.

Handling and Storing Glass

I will have more to say on this important topic in Chapter 4, *The Studio,* but the information is so vital it demands to be stated early and repeatedly.

When transporting glass by hand, small sheets are individually wrapped in newspaper and then wrapped in cardboard. Anything large (quantity or sheet size) will probably require special shipping (see details in *Buying Guide*).

In the studio, glass is carried with both hands in single sheets in an upright position. Carrying a few sheets stacked together in a flat position is very dangerous.

Glass is stored or leaned against a wall also in a nearly upright position, resting upon a stationary surface. When glass is leaned at a wide angle, it tends to slip—and it's quite dangerous to grab for sliding pieces of glass. Do not store glass overhead or stacked together in flat piles. Replace glass in its rack as soon as you've finished with it to avoid slippery piles on your workbench.

As sheets of glass accumulate, it becomes difficult to keep track of your stock and the individual colors within each rack. A glass-sample rack (construction explained in Chapter 4) will keep track of your stock, but easy location of specific colors within the racks needs a system. Either store each color separately in its own rack or combine only those colors that have a great difference, for example, red with clear, or colored antique with opal, etc. Medium to large pieces of usable scrap glass can be stored in the same way in smaller racks. Small pieces of scrap can be divided into boxes of general color group—reds in one box, blues in another, etc. Scrap smaller than three inches square is unusable for regular work and should be used immediately for practice or mosaic work, or tossed out.

Chapter 3:

TOOLS AND MATERIALS

There are four separate stages to glassworking—each with its own tools, materials, and problems. Because your tools will become a part of your hands, actually extending and specializing them, it is especially important to consider the kind of tools you will acquire and their care. (In the following list the tools and materials marked with an asterisk are most vital to the craft, and no attempt should be made to find a substitute for them.)

Ill. 3-1

Some of the basic tools and materials used in glassworking.

DESIGN
Designing Equipment (see Chapter 5)
drawing, tracing, and graph papers
rulers, triangles, and compass
black felt-tip pen and colored pencils

CUTTING
glass cutters—single edge, steel wheel
3-in-1 oil or kerosene
shallow container
large and small right triangles—plastic
    try square or straightedge—two-foot minimum
    breaking pliers
table brush or whisk broom

WRAPPING
grozing pliers (for cleaning uneven edges) and
    carbide sandpaper or grinding machine
copperfoil—six-inch-wide roll, .001 thickness
    or ¼-inch precut, self-adhesive rolls*
razor blades—single edge
masking tape—one inch wide
straightedge—metal, two feet long

SOLDERING
hammer
horseshoe nails
paintbrush—stiff bristles, ¼ inch wide
liquid flux—preferably water soluble
shallow container
solder—60/40 solid wire in rolls or
    one-pound bars*
soldering iron—heavy-duty (takes a soldering
    tip ⅜ inch in diameter)*
rasp or bastard file—flat, double-cut
tinning lid
brick or iron holder
cellulose sponge

Cutting Equipment

The recommended glass cutter is a simple, inexpensive, professional tool that will accurately score all but a very few kinds of glass.

Because the cutter is dipped into oil or kerosene before scoring the glass and may become dull or nicked by this dipping action, place a gauze pad in the bottom of a shallow container before filling it with enough liquid to cover the cutter's wheel. Replenish liquid when necessary. Damaged cutters should be replaced rather than resharpened, and therefore you should always have a few spare cutters in the studio.

The three basic guides used in cutting glass (try square, straightedge, and right triangles) must be sturdy enough to survive extended heavy use; flimsy tools need constant replacement. The guides must also be thick enough to prevent the glass cutter from riding up on the edge of the guides.

Breaking, small-plate or cut-running pliers, any of which can be used in breaking glass, should be purchased in a size that fits most comfortably in your hand.

Wrapping Equipment

For grozing pliers (used to clean the uneven edges of glass after a break) you can purchase either needle-nose pliers, tinsmith pliers or the hard-to-find grozing pliers. Tinsmith pliers are most commonly sold as grozing pliers, but they will not work as well as needle-nose or grozing pliers unless they have been detempered. Detempering makes the pliers softer and is accomplished by slowly heating and cooling the pliers in a kiln or with a butane torch. With a torch, the jaws are gradually heated until they begin to show a color change (to dull red) and then are cooled by reducing the flame gradually. The process takes fifteen to twenty minutes. Slip-joint pliers in the open position are used for breaking and in the closed position for grozing. Neither slip-joint nor needle-nose pliers need be detempered. Breaking pliers can also be used for grozing.

A grinding machine can replace these grozing tools, but it is expensive and therefore more suitable for a commercial studio than for beginning work. If you do become seriously involved with glasswork, it's a necessary luxury. (DO NOT try using an electric drill with a grinding attachment; it doesn't work and is very dangerous.) A belt grinder with a silicon-carbide abrasive wheel and a minimum of 3,000 RPM will do the job quite well.

Rolls of copperfoil are sold in a variety of sheet thicknesses. A thickness of .001 inch is suitable for most work, but you may want to try a heavier (thicker) foil for very large structures. A metal straightedge is the best guide to use when cutting copperfoil, because it will survive the occasional biting of the razor into its edge. Anything less resistant will be damaged quickly. The straightedge should measure at least two feet long in order to obtain foil strips of the required length. Razors rather than scissors are used to cut foil, because of their ability to slice a cleaner, straighter edge.

Soldering Equipment

Flat horseshoe nails (also called glazing nails), used for surrounding the unsoldered panel during the tacking process, hold the glass edge much better than round nails.

Different formulas for liquid flux will affect the way in which the molten solder flows and the corrosive action on the copper tip of your soldering iron. The choice is either to experiment with commercial brands or to mix your own. An excellent formula for liquid flux is: one part hydrochloric acid to seven parts glycerin; mix well and store in plastic half-gallon jugs. NOTE: flux is poisonous; fumes should be avoided and skin contact limited.

Solder consists of different quantities of mixed metals. Each kind of solder is used for a specific job—electrical, plumbing, etc. The best solder for copperfoil work is 60/40 solid wire solder, sold in one-pound rolls or bars. The numbers mean that the solder contains 60 percent tin and 40 percent lead. Always make sure to buy solder in these proportions. Do *not* use 60 percent lead and 40 percent tin solder. The solid wire is important also; do not use a solder with a rosin or acid core. Always have at least two rolls of solder on hand. You can save the end bits from each roll and use them by holding the small lengths with a pair of pliers and soldering as usual. Solder will only adhere to a fluxed metal—never to clothing, glass, wood, etc. When cooled, drops may be picked off these surfaces by hand.

A good soldering iron is one of the more important, expensive, and hard-to-find tools of the craft. The care you give to your iron will determine how well and how long it will function. Because many irons do not come with complete cleaning and tinning instructions or maintenance information, use the following as a guide:

(1) use only rated voltage,
(2) keep the cord free of knots and kinks,
(3) never immerse the tip in liquids,
(4) maintain control over the iron's heating and cooling,
(5) never rap the iron against hard objects,
(6) keep the tip well cleaned and tinned at all times,
(7) periodically remove the tip and clean its shaft and shank,
(8) keep the tip-screw tight and the tip well inserted in its shaft.

Some of the above points require further explanation. To control the heating and cooling of your iron, attach an on/off switch to the cord or plug the iron into a voltage regulator (rheostat). Without such controls, the tip of the iron will heat to more than twice the temperature needed to melt solder. This overheating will cause the solder to melt through to the side opposite the one on which you are working. Also, the burning flux will corrode the tip excessively. Constant heating and inadequate cleaning will cause the tip almost to become welded in its shaft, requiring a pair of pliers and some elbow grease to remove the tip for cleaning. All of the above will shorten the life of your soldering iron.

Part of regular soldering work involves cleaning and tinning the iron's tip at the end of each day's work. This job is explained in the soldering section of Chapter 6, but instructions for periodic cleaning and for making a tinning lid are best explained here. To remove excess solder from the tip (while you are working and the tip is hot), wipe the tip with a cellulose sponge or damp cloth or shake off the excess. Never rap the iron against the workbench to remove solder, because this will damage the iron's heating element. In order to remove the carbon deposits that collect along the inner wall of the tip's shaft, the iron must be cold and unplugged with the tip-screw and tip removed. Clean the shaft by scraping the wall with any long metal rod, screwdriver, or file. Before replacing the tip, shake out scrapings and file the tip shank to a bright copper. Proper contact with the heating element will only occur if the tip is well inserted into its shaft before you tighten the holding screw (tip-screw). Always rest the iron on a brick or in a special iron holder when it is hot.

To make a tinning lid, nail a jar lid to a piece of lath or to a thin block of wood. This will permit you to hold and maneuver the lid while tinning. Otherwise, the lid would become too hot to handle. The tinning lid should hold about ½ teaspoon of flux and a one- or two-inch strip of solder that is used to tin the copper tip on the soldering iron. These materials should be replenished when necessary.

If you are ambitious, you may make your own copper tips. Purchase a solid copper rod that is slightly thinner than the diameter of the tip's shaft, and saw off the desired length. This piece may then be filed and bent to almost any shape that your soldering work requires—round, bevel, chisel, semichisel, etc. The pyramid-shaped copper tip, however, which is often supplied with the iron, works quite adequately when filed to a smooth, rounded shape.

Chapter 4:

THE STUDIO

The Studio as a Controlled Environment

The exact arrangement and function of a studio depends upon a critical understanding of self, the medium, and its needs—and how to relate this information to the available space. Ill. 4-1 should be used as a general guide and combined with the following description to form a framework in which to design your studio. A studio can fluctuate from a good-sized work board to a full working studio, depending upon your personal resources. But for serious glassworking you will need the following equipment:

workbench
light box
glass racks
sample rack
grinding machine
waste disposal
shelves
drawing table
chair
peg board
overhead lighting
windows
tools
materials

The relationship that exists between you and your work should not be interrupted by unnecessary forms and objects. Whereas curtains, rugs, or fabric-covered chairs often are distracting, even hazardous additions, reference books, plants, and music seem to blend well with a studio and even heighten the pleasure of working. A good studio has the feeling of airiness, light, space, and Shaker-like simplicity. It is a room of singular purpose and needs light-reflecting, bright walls; a smooth, safe floor; open, unadorned windows; and uniform overhead lighting.

Light, both direct and reflected, is *essential* to the craft. The richest source is natural light that brings out all the hidden color changes, bubbles, striations, and other imperfections that are found in beautiful glass. For this reason—and also for adequate ventilation—your studio must have at least one large window. With a light color on your walls, natural and incandescent light is intensified and aids both glassworking and cleaning of the studio. When daylight is available, use it in conjunction with a light box. While the box will give you a biased reading of color, it is your best working light at night (when colors cannot be cross-examined in natural light), and its hard, smooth glass top is an excellent cutting surface. A light box is not essential to begin glasswork, but without it you will almost be unable to examine six or eight colors as they relate to each other.

Wood is used exclusively in the studio for safety as well as control. It has the ability to give without loss of strength, and it also disperses the excessive heat that results from soldering. In comparison, metal—though harder than wood—increases the dangers of breakage by its rigidity, and it retains heat, which makes it a poor base for soldering. Therefore, all studio furniture should be of wooden construction.

Glass racks may vary in size and shape, depending upon the kinds of glass they hold. However designed, they should be only slightly larger in height than the actual sheets of glass. You can mount a peg board on the sides of your glass racks to hold your tools for easy access.

Ill. 4-1

A glassworking studio empty *(top)* and equipped *(below);* this size studio is one of the many possible compromises between a full working studio and a portable one.

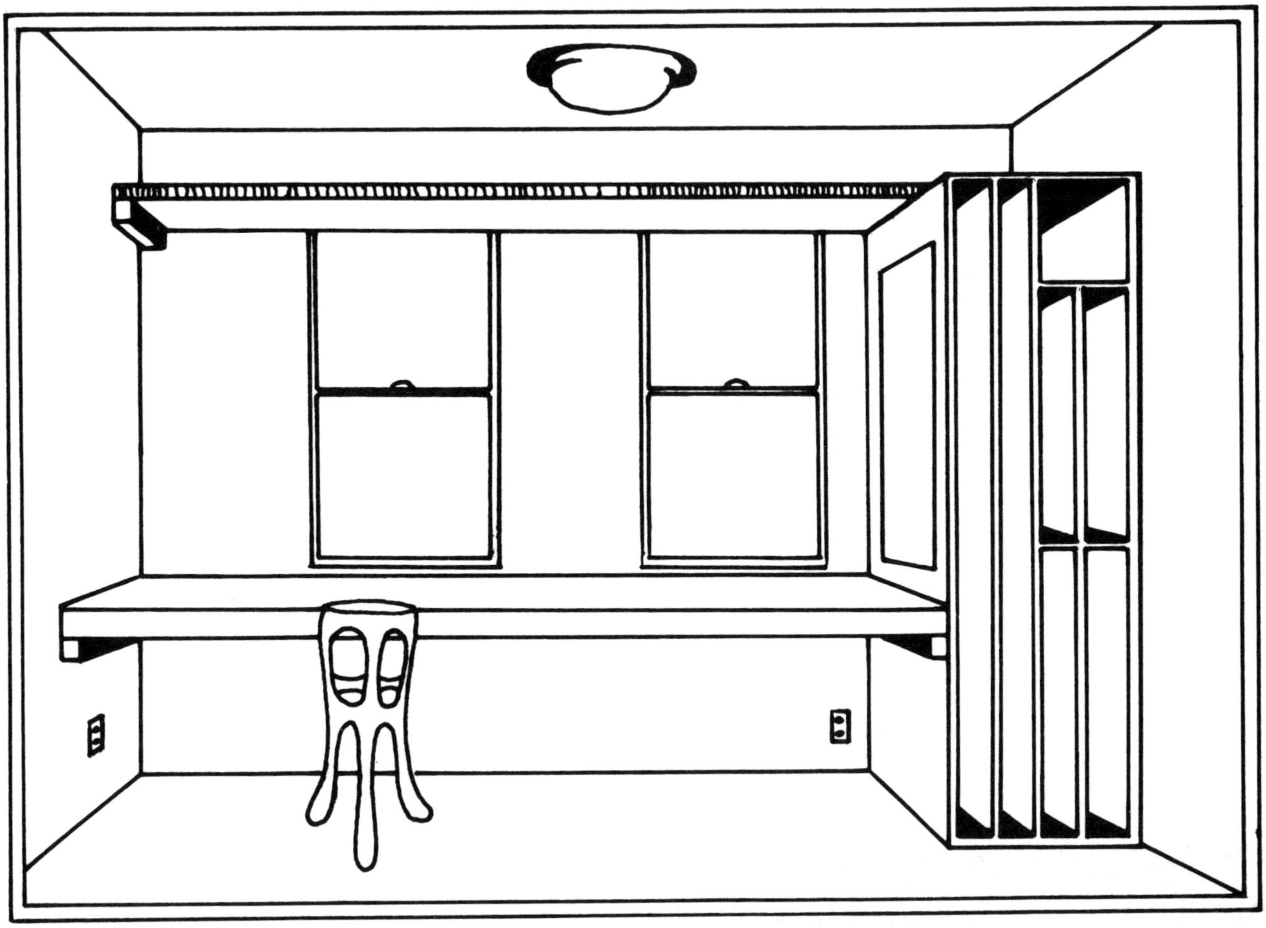

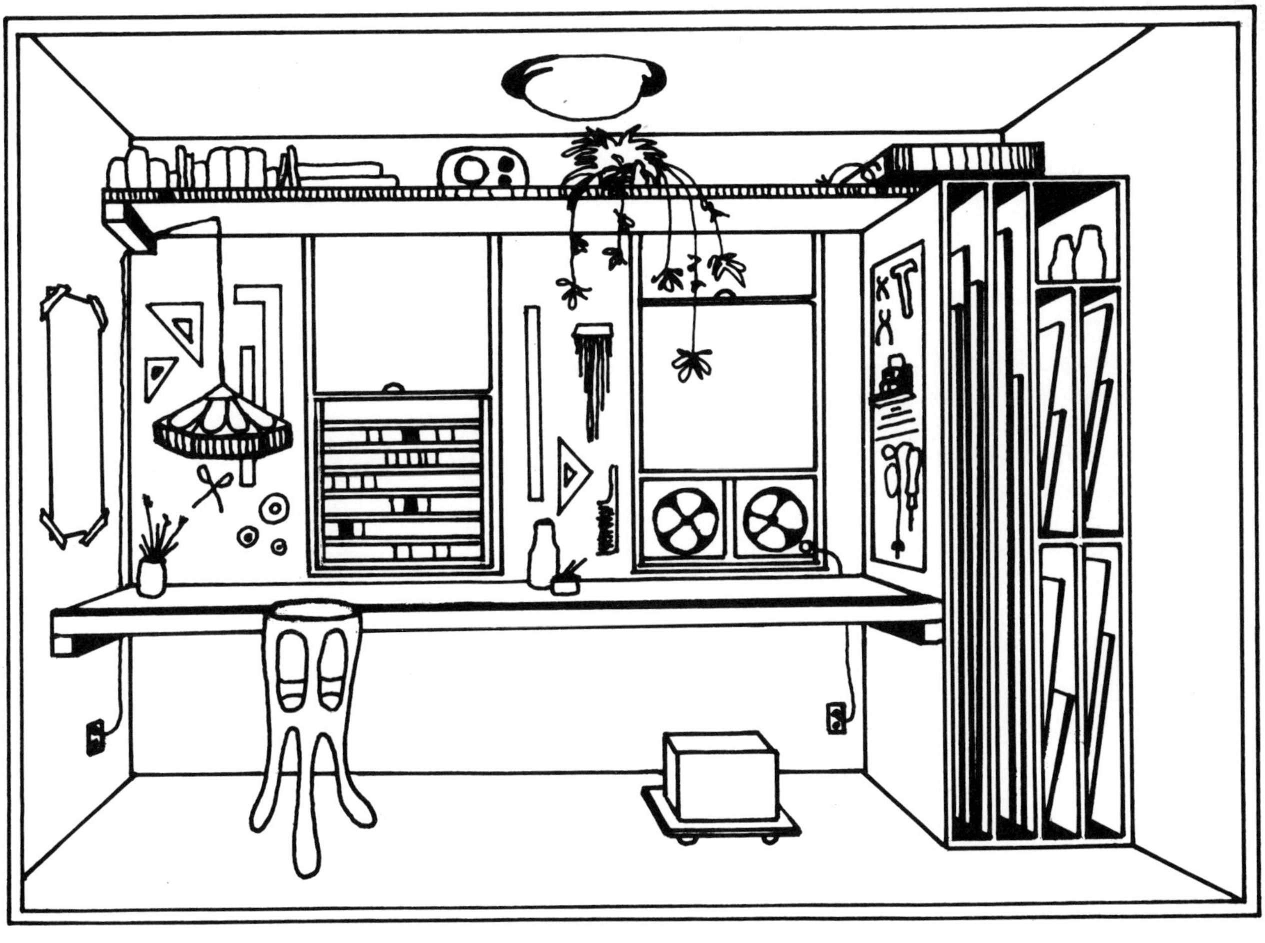

Placement of furniture will vary somewhat with each studio, although there are certain similarities of arrangement that apply to all. The ideal workbench is either freestanding or with one short end attached to a wall. In either case, the bench must be solid enough to support your weight leaning against it without tipping or wobbling, and it should be located in the center of activity with glass, tools, materials, and waste disposal close at hand. You can use the bench for all work stages, of course. However, by separating design and foil preparation from the cutting, grozing, wrapping, and soldering stages, you ensure legible drawings and clean foil. If you have the room, separate cutting work from soldering work by using two workbenches rather than one.

If you have a grinding machine, mount it within a few feet of the workbench, not on the bench itself—otherwise, the vibration set up by the spinning wheel will "walk" glass sheets off the surface.

As waste glass accumulates, it becomes too heavy for normal disposal. You can collect it in a medium-sized cardboard carton that has a padding of newspaper on its bottom. Rest the box on a dolly so you can move it easily around the studio.

If you have only a tentative interest in glass or an extreme shortage of space, adjustments in these recommendations can be made to suit your needs. But the dangers and discomforts of glassworking will increase as your working space decreases. So exercise extra care when working in a small work area.

Portable Studio

Practically all of the equipment needed for a permanent studio will be needed also for a portable studio. The portable workbench is a piece of ½-inch plywood, measuring approximately two and a half by three feet, which you place on a solid desk or table. Tools, glass, and materials can all be stored in a closet or a large box—preferably locked, especially if children are around. Waste glass must be disposed of immediately as part of your regular refuse and not be allowed to accumulate. While you are working, pull back all rugs and move fabric chairs far away from the work area. Cleanup must be extrameticulous with a portable studio.

Although this is not an ideal arrangement, it will enable you to make many stained glassworks that would otherwise only be possible in a permanently set-up studio.

Safety

The fact that glass is a dangerous medium can never be overlooked. However, it is generally not the dramatic act of carrying a large sheet of glass that results in bodily harm; cuts usually come about in a more insidious way, such as leaning upon invisible splinters of glass on a work surface. For personal safety, wear closed shoes, work goggles (or—if you do not wear eyeglasses—lightly tinted sunglasses), close-fitting but comfortable clothes, and, if you like, a work apron.

For the safety of friends, children, and pets, arrange your studio so that it is not an integral part of a living room. Glass and all its related tools and materials demand an area of their own, because nearly everything involved is either poisonous, sharp, or hot.

Adequate safety precautions, working room, excellent tools, and materials are a major part —but not the whole part—of studio comfort. Physical and mental ease are also important work factors. The semitrance that often accompanies the close concentration of glassworking is great for the mind but wreaks subtle havoc on the body. Glassworkers tend to be an achy lot. Remember to stretch, yawn, and keep a window open to avoid fume headaches. Occasionally wash your face and drink some water to stop dehydration. Flux and solder make for dirty hands; use professional hand cleaners with a scrub brush and follow up with a good hand cream to keep your hands from drying out. In general, keep in mind that any confinement will affect your work adversely and that discomfort will not always be apparent until after you have tried the alternative.

Studio Furniture

The workbench—used for cutting, wrapping, and soldering work—is a wooden table with a surface area that measures three feet in width and a minimum of five feet in length. Glassworkers often prefer a bench that reaches to just below their rib cages, but a normal desk or table height is also acceptable. Whether you build, buy, or alter a workbench, always nail a strip of lath along the length of the work surface at the bench's edge. This strip creates a permanent straight edge that prevents sheets of glass from sliding off the surface, and it is especially useful during cutting and soldering work. The work surface of the bench can be left as plain wood or partially covered with felt. Felt makes an excellent cutting surface, but it is useless for soldering work, because the cloth soon becomes covered with greasy flux and bits of solder. If you want to use felt, your workbench must be long enough to allow you to cut on one section and solder on another. To separate these two functions, your bench should measure about eight feet long. If this is the case, cover half the work surface with a tightly wrapped, double thickness of felt and nail or staple it down securely. (Make sure that the nails or staples are not on the work surface, because they will crack and chip glass.) The lath strip is then nailed over the felt and continued on to the end of the bench.

The light box—used as a glass-cutting surface and for examining different colors of glass—consists of a box of variable dimensions, a light source, and a top of thick plate glass. The design options are variable, since a light box's size depends upon working capital (plate glass is expensive), the kind of lighting you choose to employ (natural, incandescent, or fluorescent), and whether you prefer a portable or permanent light box. By understanding the basics of the portable box, you can apply the same information to the permanent box.

A portable light box measures approximately two feet long, two feet wide, and one foot deep (from top of glass to work surface). The top is a recessed sheet of clear or frosted ¼-inch plate glass, approximately two feet square. The rest of the box consists of four wooden sides nailed into four wooden legs. For ventilation purposes, the box does not have a bottom, and the sides do not extend to the work surface. For lighting, the simplest solution is to mount one or more porcelain fixtures six inches below the glass top (to avoid cracking the glass with heat), and use regular low-watt light bulbs or fluorescent lamps.

Such a portable light box is one good solution to limited studio space. It can be assembled and disassembled at will; when you are not using the box, its frame can be hung on the wall and the glass top stored separately. When constructing a light box, you can recess the glass by cutting a ¼-inch groove into the top edge of the supporting structure with a router, by simply resting the glass upon the four legs (with legs nailed to a height ¼ inch below the surface level), or by adding wooden supports ¼ inch below the surface level along the length and width of the frame. You must use glue and screws to secure such supports, or they will not be capable of supporting plate glass. To increase and spread your light, place a sheet of tin beneath the box on your bench's work surface. If you cannot locate frosted plate glass and want to reduce light-bulb glare, spray the underside of the clear plate with a thin coat of enamel frosting.

A permanent light box is made by removing a large square from your workbench surface, replacing it with a recessed sheet of plate glass, and mounting lighting fixtures six inches beneath the glass surface. If your light box is larger than two feet square, you must add a center support across it underneath the glass so that the glass is supported adequately.

It is especially important when planning the major pieces of studio furniture—workbench and light box—that you consider all the alternatives and, if need be, invent your own solutions.

Glass racks are used simply for storage. Glass should never be stored flat but always lengthwise in an upright position in sturdy wooden racks. If you order glass by the crate, simply empty the crate, upend it, nail it to the floor, wall, and ceiling (if possible), and then replace the glass within the crate (minus packing materials). Each new shipment of glass will extend your racks. If you build your own racks, keep them as small as possible (preferably below head level) and sturdy (use two-by-fours and ¼-inch plywood). Be sure to place wooden dividers every six or eight inches. Wooden milk crates upended and nailed to the floor and wall are sufficient for medium-to-large-size scrap pieces. Milk crates—with a lining of cardboard stapled to their inner walls and bottom to prevent pieces from slipping out—are excellent for collecting small scrap. You many want to attach wheels to these boxes.

In order to keep track of the colors and kinds of glass you have as your stock accumulates, you will need a sample rack. There are several different ways to display glass, but one simple, flexible method is to cut a three-inch-by-two-inch rectangle from each large sheet of glass and mount these upon a piece of plate glass with blobs of plasticine. The plate glass, which should measure about one-half of your window size, can then be leaned or mounted in your studio window. This method will allow you to remove a sample of glass that you no longer have in stock and to add new samples without undue difficulty.

Shop Yoga

The philosophy of yoga involves an intense self-awareness not only through bodily discipline but also through deep, reflective understanding. Shop yoga can aid the transfer of creative thought into artistic fact. The goal should be a correct relationship between thinking and working—not just the finished piece.

In order to understand—and therefore control—the craft, you must be aware not only of the sights, sounds, smells, and feel of glasswork but also of the history and mystery that surround it.

Glass has all the paradox of an ice cube; it is a molasses-like liquid that is worked and used in a hard, brittle form. Although glass is virtually indestructible—that is, nonbiodegradable—centuries of standing in an upright position, such as in old cathedral windows, will cause it to flow. Each piece in the window will become perceptibly thinner on top and thicker on the bottom.

The oldest specimen of sheet glass dates back to ancient Egypt—some 2,000 years before the Christian era. Five hundred years later, a fully evolved glass industry thrived in Egypt. In all the intervening millennia, manufacturing techniques have changed so little that an ancient Egyptian would feel quite at home in a modern-day glassblowing factory.

Nature—unaided by man—can produce glass; in Yellowstone National Park there is an entire mountain of a natural glass called obsidian. This same black, volcanic glass was so precious to ancient man that one of the world's oldest cities, Çatal Hüyük in Anatolia, owed much of its success to a nearby source of obsidian. And at the other end of our history, the astronauts on Apollo 11 found and brought back a similar form of natural glass from their walk on the moon.

Apart from its rather exotic history—of which the above is but a mere sampling—glass also continually surprises its users with very strange happenings. Glass will speak to you. It will teach you the correct pressure it needs for cutting if you listen to the faint, plastic, zipper-like sound of the score. This sound will tell you how the glass is going to break—clean, jagged, or completely askew. The tension that builds along the score line even before the breaking can be felt in your fingertips. Glass also seems to defy the laws of physics, in that you appear to hear a clean break before you see it part like water in slow motion.

Sense awareness is such an integral part of glassworking that even after a sheet has been approved by instrument, a distributor will tap the sheet and listen to the sound of the vibrations before he gives it his final approval. In fact, after some time of glassworking, you will be able to judge well-tempered glass from poorly tempered glass simply by holding it in your hands. Ill-tempered glass will have a strained feeling to it—its molecules being at odds with one another—while well-tempered glass will lie restful and secure in your hands.

Handling large sheets of glass is comparable to moving nitroglycerin; it can sometimes take an incredible amount of abuse, but if it has a slight flaw or run at its edge, the smallest jar can divide the sheet with guillotine speed.

While the various odors of glassworking—to be honest—can be fairly unpleasant, a particularly bad or strong smell is generally a warning that bears investigation. In particular, the burning smell that occurs just before a piece of glass shatters at the grinding wheel should be heeded, as should the piercing odor of improperly mixed flux.

As your senses become attuned to this new activity, your speed will increase along with the rise in your craft level. The distance between yourself and the medium decreases as the relation between yourself and what you are doing intensifies. Anything that reinforces the inseparableness of the creator and the created should be sought as part of an enlightened way of working—and that is what is meant by the term *shop yoga.*

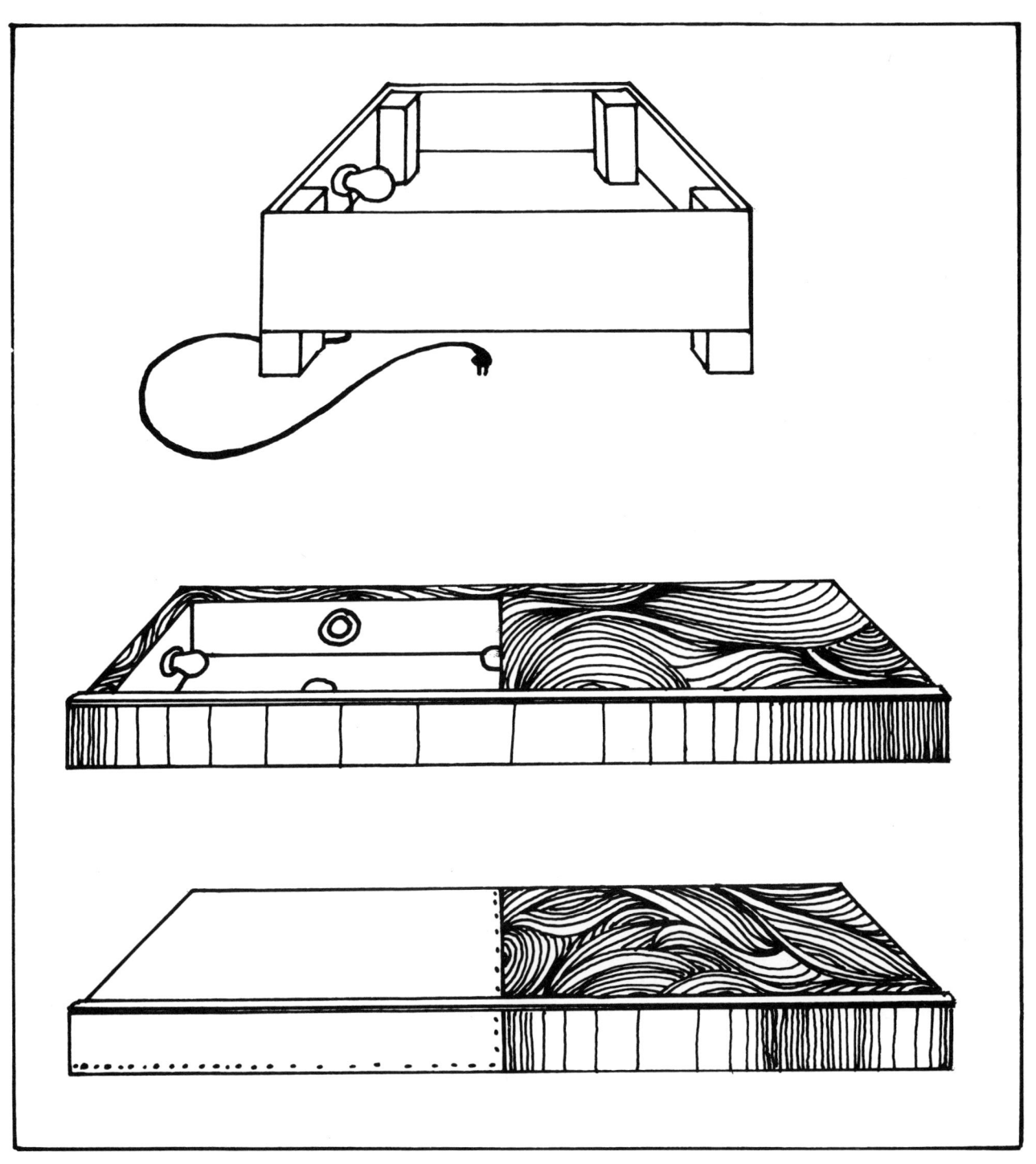

Ill. 4-2

A portable light box, a permanent light box (built into the workbench surface), and a workbench surface partially covered with felt.

Chapter 5:

APPLIED DESIGN

The idea behind this design chapter is to take you through the basic design problems of a practice panel of glass—without patronizing you as a beginner. Therefore, rather than insert a completed design here for you to copy, a fast solution that teaches nothing, I will let you work out your own designs.

In glass designing it makes no great difference where or how you begin, although it is an indisputable fact that a straight line is easier to cut than a curved line and that many shapes you can conceive simply cannot be cut in glass. Listing each subtle difference between what is and what is not possible in glass and each possible solution would be an endless waste of time.

The excitement of glass is in color, light, texture, and change. Technique is mostly a chore to be learned, mastered, and relegated to a proficient state of second nature. Save your more elaborate design ideas until after you have gone through the actual step-by-step design routine from beginning to end, and you will have a better perspective on designing possibilities. Beginning with small, imitative/representational works—sailboats, small birds, and other gewgaws—will teach you much less than the progression.

The use of progressions is a solution for eliminating impossible cuts and an aid to three-dimensional design. The following formula, in mathematical terms, is a descending, geometric progression with alternating divisions of equal areas. In simply stated directions: take a square and divide it in half, then divide all or some of the resulting spaces in half, and again divide all or some of the resulting spaces in half. These divisions can be horizontal or vertical. The progression can be stopped at any point; that decision is an arbitrary and personal one. It can be manipulated through space on a three-dimensional plane, as if you were designing a box. Ills. 5-1 to 5-5 are design examples following the above formula for a 1:2 progression. They have been shaded to suggest color and to simplify "reading" the changes.

The concept of a progression—a logical movement from one step to another—invites applying it to other forms and dimensions. Because all of the examples have been intentionally limited to a 1:2 relationship, they constitute only a fraction of their designing possibilities. It is for you to discover the progressions possible within colors, circles, and triangles. Try a 1:3 ratio alone or combined with a 1:2 proportion. If you like, you can find proportional inspiration in the rhythm of music and poetry and in the spatial relationships of architecture and painting.

To practice progressions, lay out four boxes of the same size on a piece of graph paper and work out four different progressions. Repeat this process until you have twelve different designs on three separate pages of graph paper. This will allow you a fair set of alternatives from which you can choose.

When sketching designs, use double lines and shade in some areas that will imitate and help you to visualize the finished glass panel. Once you choose a final design, draw it to size on graph paper, using a single black line. All designs should be made in triplicate. Retain the original drawing as a record of your work, use one copy for cutting the glass, and lay

Ill. 5-1

The step-by-step workings of a design progression up through the bottom left-hand box; the bottom right-hand box is a finished design after nine more lines have been added in the same manner.

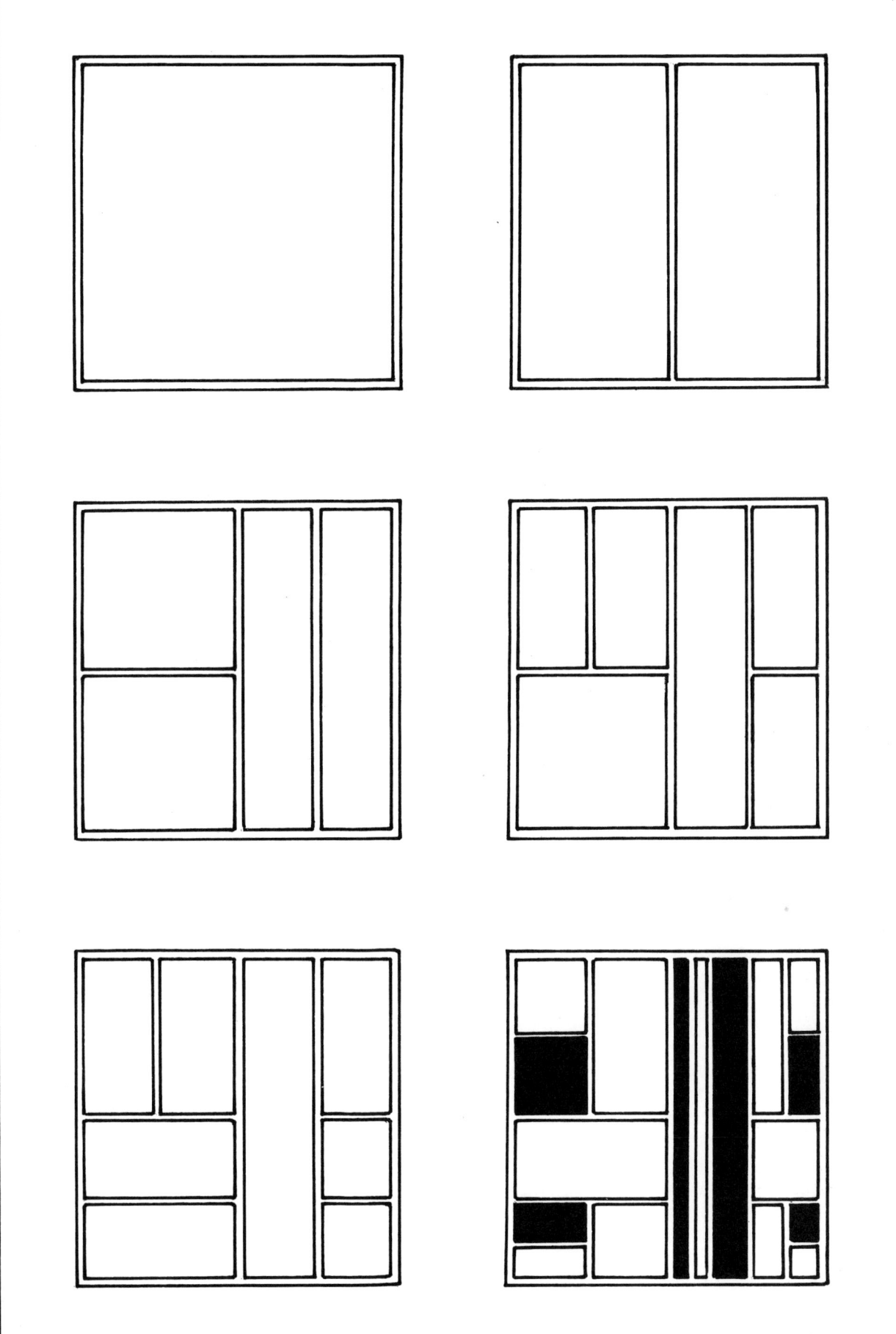

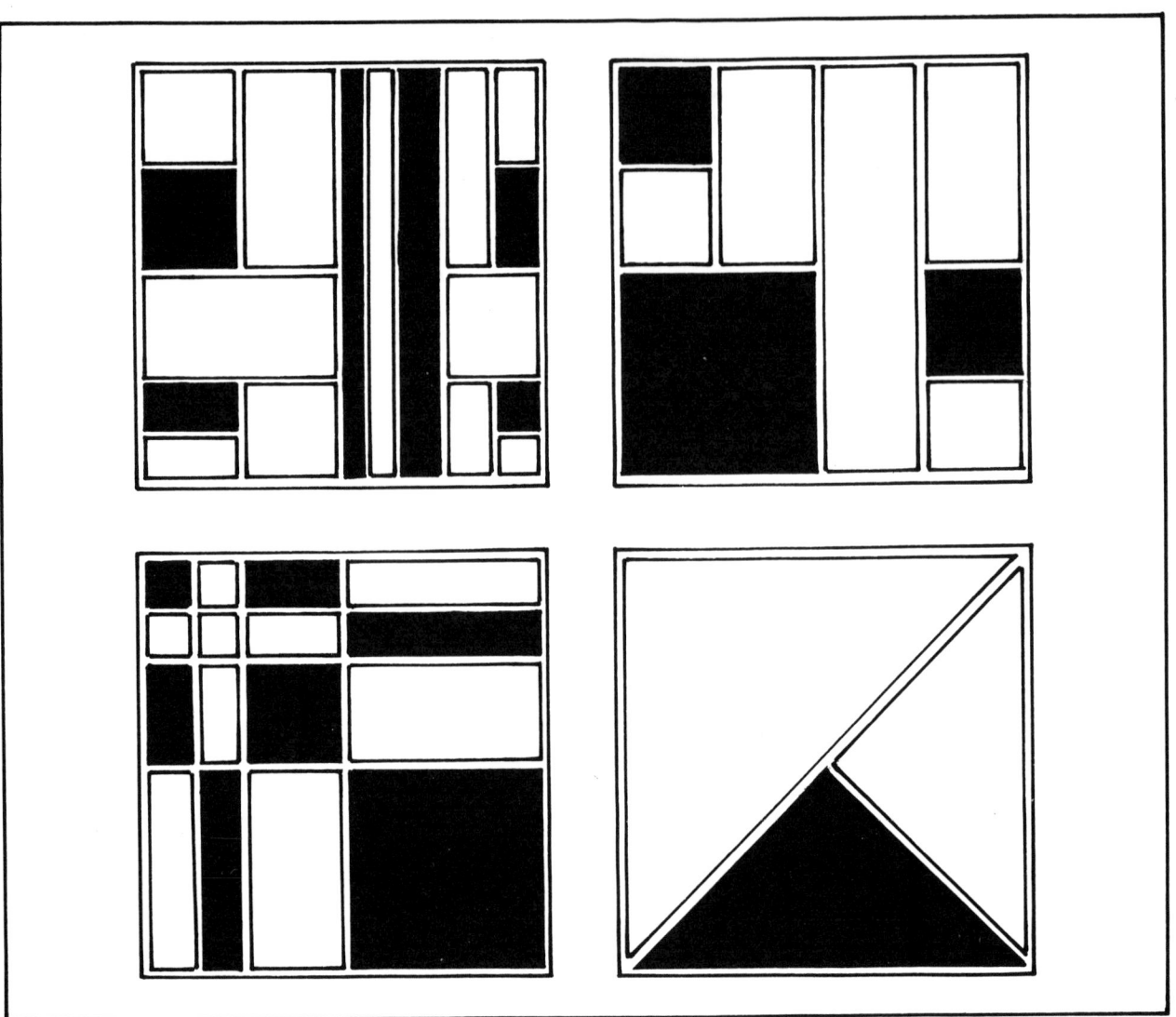

out the other copy for the immediate transfer of cut pieces to their proper positions. All three drawings should be color-coded—R for red, R-O for reddish-orange, etc. The two working drawings, which should be on a heavy vellum tracing paper, must be especially accurate.

For your first glass panel, work out a progression design of eight or ten pieces with the perimeter measuring approximately six inches square. Use light-colored, imported antique glass of high transparency, which is easy to cut and whose colors can be appreciated even without a light box. Place the glass directly over the drawing and commence cutting (see Chapter 6). Plan your cuts; if you will only be using a quarter of a sheet of glass, remove this section from the full sheet before cutting out the individual pieces. Otherwise, if a break runs wild, a good portion of the sheet will be lost. Planning keeps scrap to a minimum and ensures that you have enough glass of a specific color to recut a shape.

Ill. 5-2 *(above)*

Four different examples of the 1:2 progression.

Ill. 5-3 →

A turning progression; at top, the direction of the turn; at center, the result of quarter turns in a clockwise direction on a line; at bottom left, the result of quarter turns in a clockwise direction on a pivot; and at bottom right, the result of a counter-clockwise direction on a pivot.

Ill. 5-4 *(page 34)*

A progression as it extends into a three-dimensional box *(top),* and its components separated on a two-dimensional plane.

Ill. 5-5 *(page 35)*

A progression as it translates from a square to a trapezoid and into lamp parts.

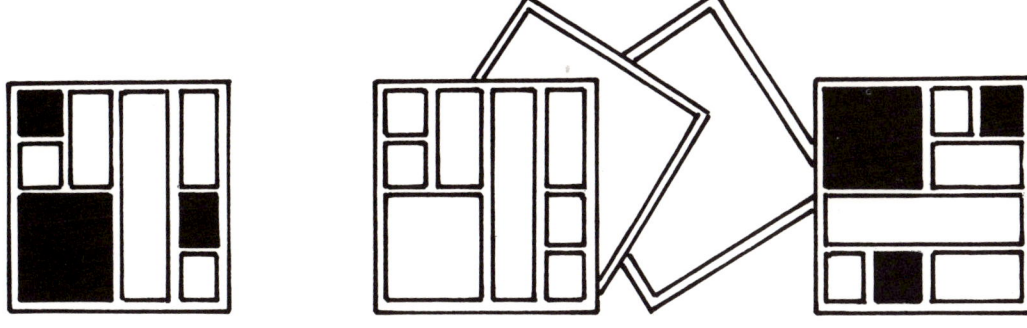
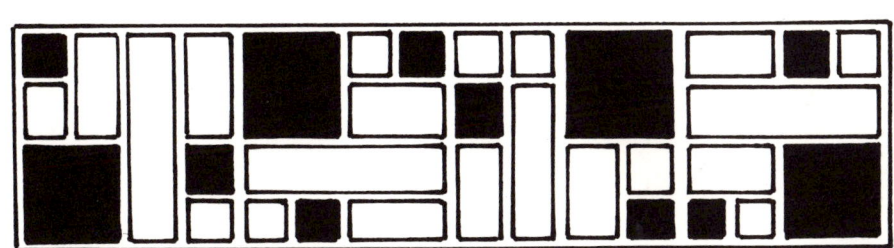

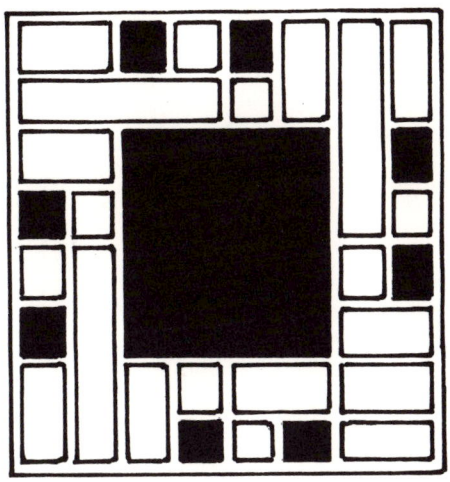

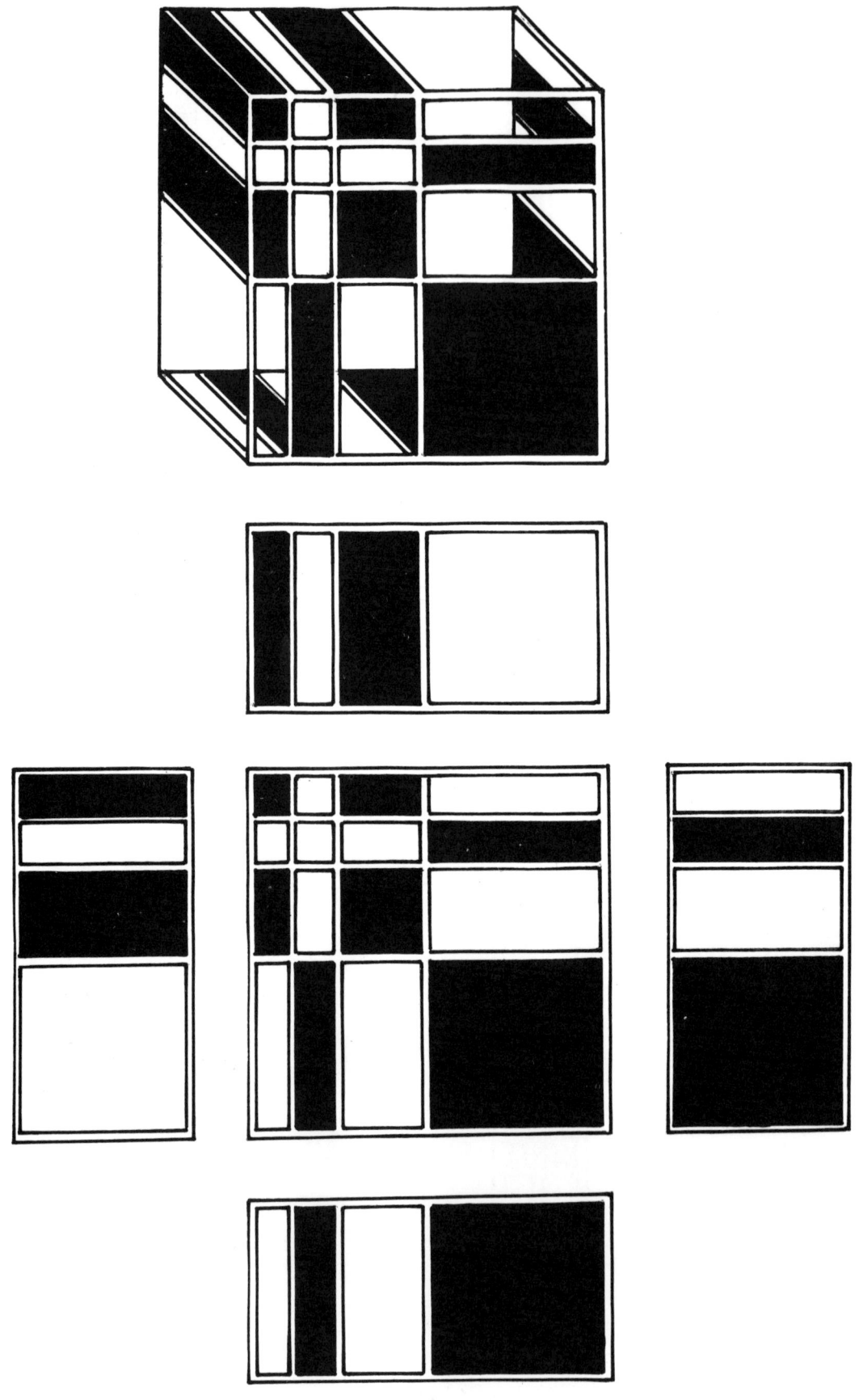

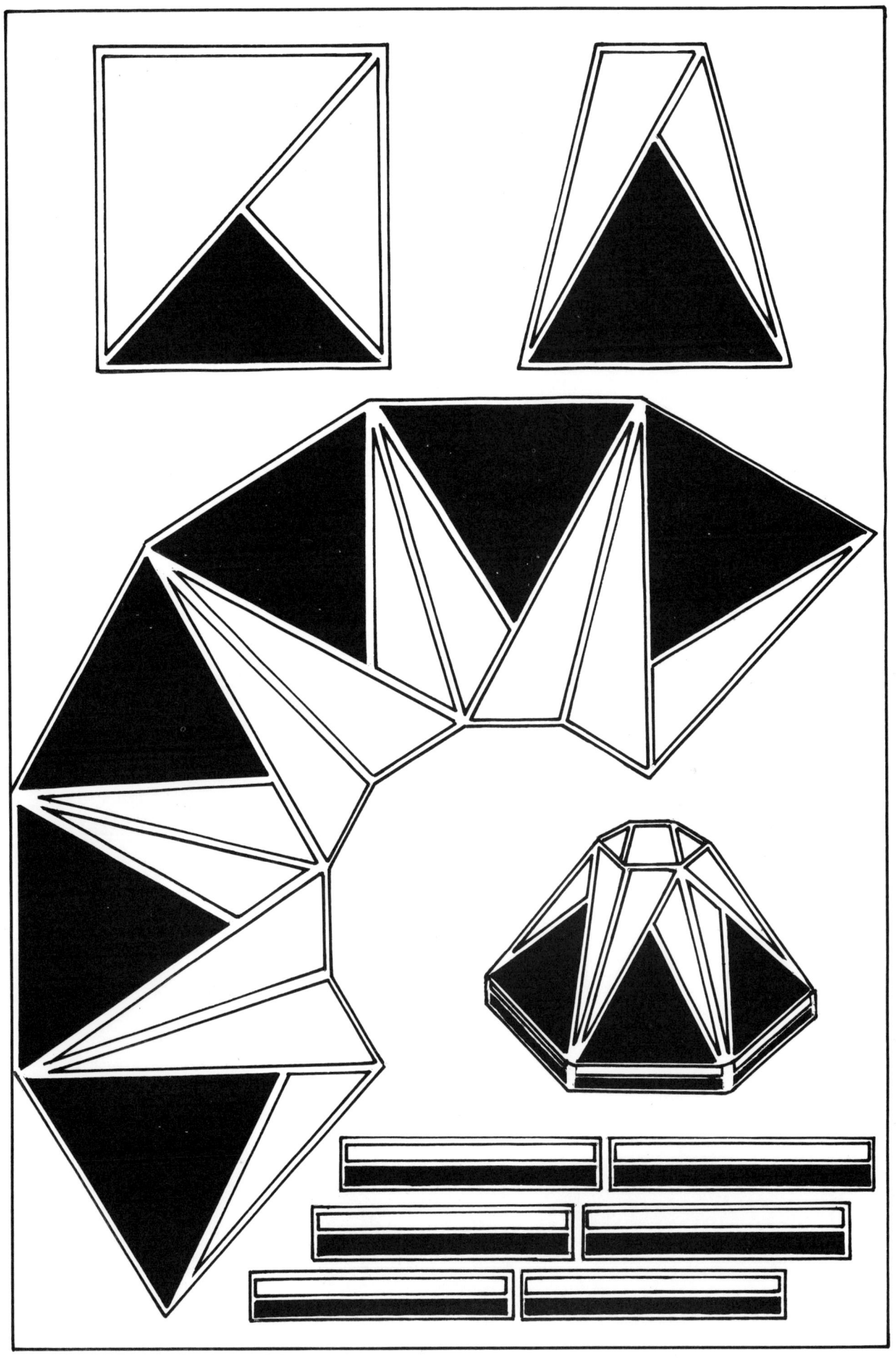

Some Impossible Cuts and Their Solutions

With a series of intricate cuts, a deeply curved line may be cut into glass, but it is impossible —even for a master—to cut an angle greater than 180° so that it wraps around a corner. This must be considered when you are not working with progressions. In Ills. 5-6 to 5-9 this problem—represented with a triangle and a square—is first illustrated *(top left)* and then resolved with vertical *(top right)*, horizontal *(bottom left)*, and diagonal *(bottom right)* solutions. It is interesting to note how each solution changes the entire look of the design. This also points up the fact that all lead lines in a completed design are not there strictly for beauty but are often the result of the glassworker complying with the demands and limitations of the glass.

Ills. 5-6 to 5-9

Four impossible cuts and their solutions. In each of these illustrations, the top-left drawing presents the problem cut, the top-right drawing is a vertical solution; the bottom-left, a horizontal solution; and the bottom-right, a diagonal solution.

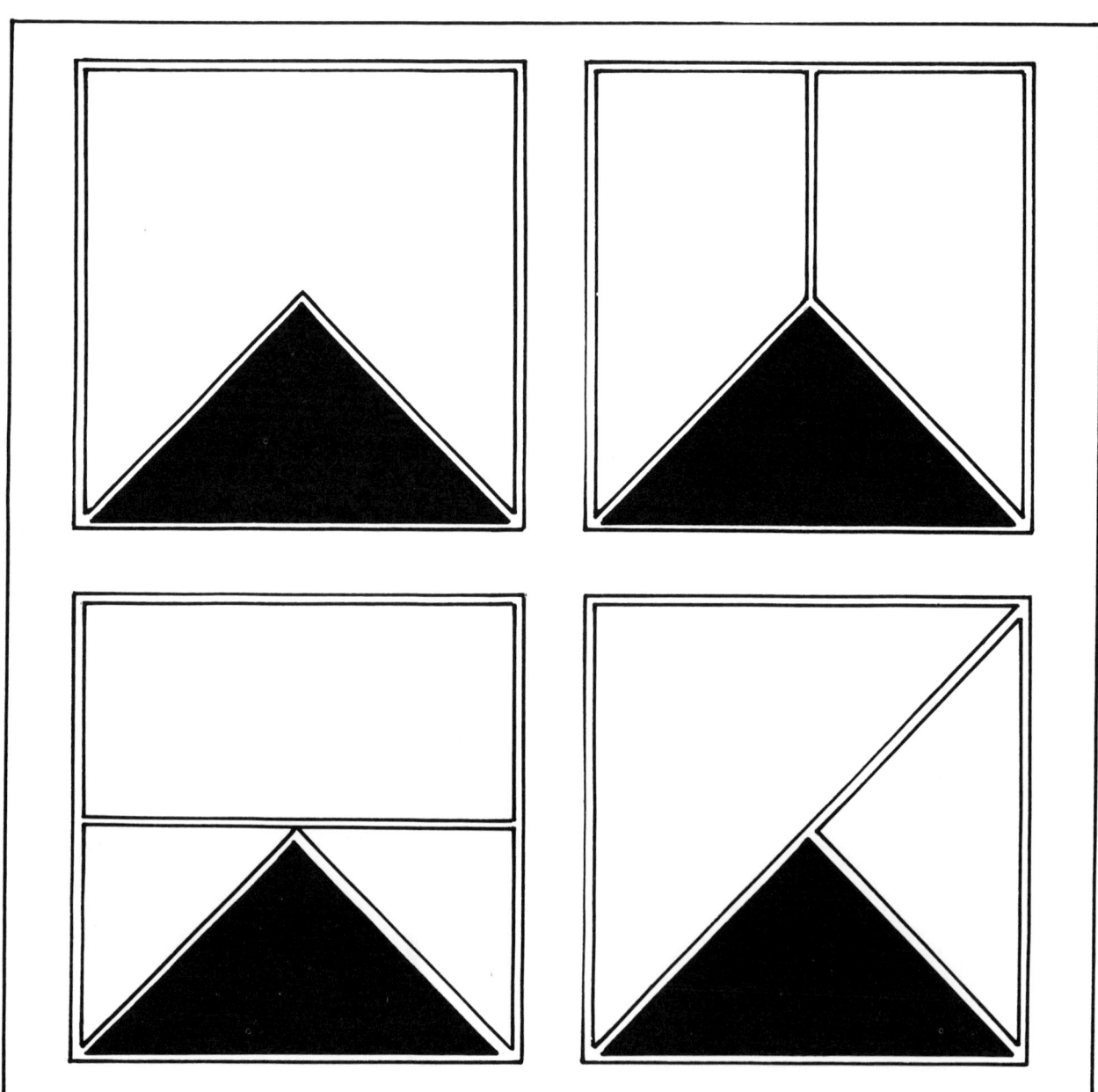

Chapter 6:
MANUAL

Now we get down to work—the actual step-by-step process of glassworking. Once you complete the design and choose the glass and color-code your drawings, here is the general sequence for glassworking:
(1) prepare your tools and cutting area,
(2) cut the glass and assemble the pieces on the work surface,
(3) remove cutting discrepancies by grozing to ensure a more perfect fit,
(4) cut strips of copperfoil and prepare the soldering area,
(5) wrap each piece of glass in copperfoil and reassemble the design on the work surface,
(6) flux and solder the entire work—both faces and the perimeter,
(7) attach hanging loops or other hardware to the perimeter,
(8) scrub the completed work,
(9) clean, tin, and store your soldering iron,
(10) clean and clear your work area.
The important phases of each of these steps make up the rest of this chapter. Many of these details are absolutely vital to understanding and mastering the craft of glassworking. If, on the first reading, they seem complex, do not panic; once you begin the actual work, you will see the logic of each step, and the whole process will be immediately simplified.

Cutting

The first step is to gather together all your cutting tools on your work surface. You will need the following:
glass cutter
3-in-1 oil or kerosene
shallow container
large and small triangles
try square
breaking pliers
table brush or whisk broom

Before you begin cutting glass for a specific design, it is always a good idea to warm up with practice cuts on scrap glass. Once you begin work on the actual design, place the glass you are cutting directly over one copy of the design. The second copy is placed off to one side of the cutting area, within arm's reach, for easy assembly of the design.

The glass cutter is held in what will seem, at first, a very unnatural position. *It must be held between the fore and middle fingers, with the thumb pressing from behind,* as if you were about to take a pinch of salt (Ill. 6-1). Make sure that before you score, the work surface and glass are clean, because debris underneath glass will cause it to break prematurely and dust on the glass will interfere with scoring. Stand over the glass to score, dip the cutter into oil or kerosene, slide the cutter *up* the glass without pressure, and then *down* the same track with enough pressure to scratch the glass. When the cutter is slid up the glass, it will leave behind a trail of oil that is used as a guide for coming back down the glass. The pressure on the cutter remains constant from beginning to end. The motion of scoring is a smooth, fluid one, without any hesitation or backtracking.

Generally, make the score on the smoothest side of the glass—the one with the highest shine and the fewest imperfections. Always test, however, to see which side produces the easiest, cleanest score, because there are exceptions to this general rule. For example, imported antique glass is often scored on the textured side for best results.

Ill. 6-1

The proper way to hold the glass cutter.

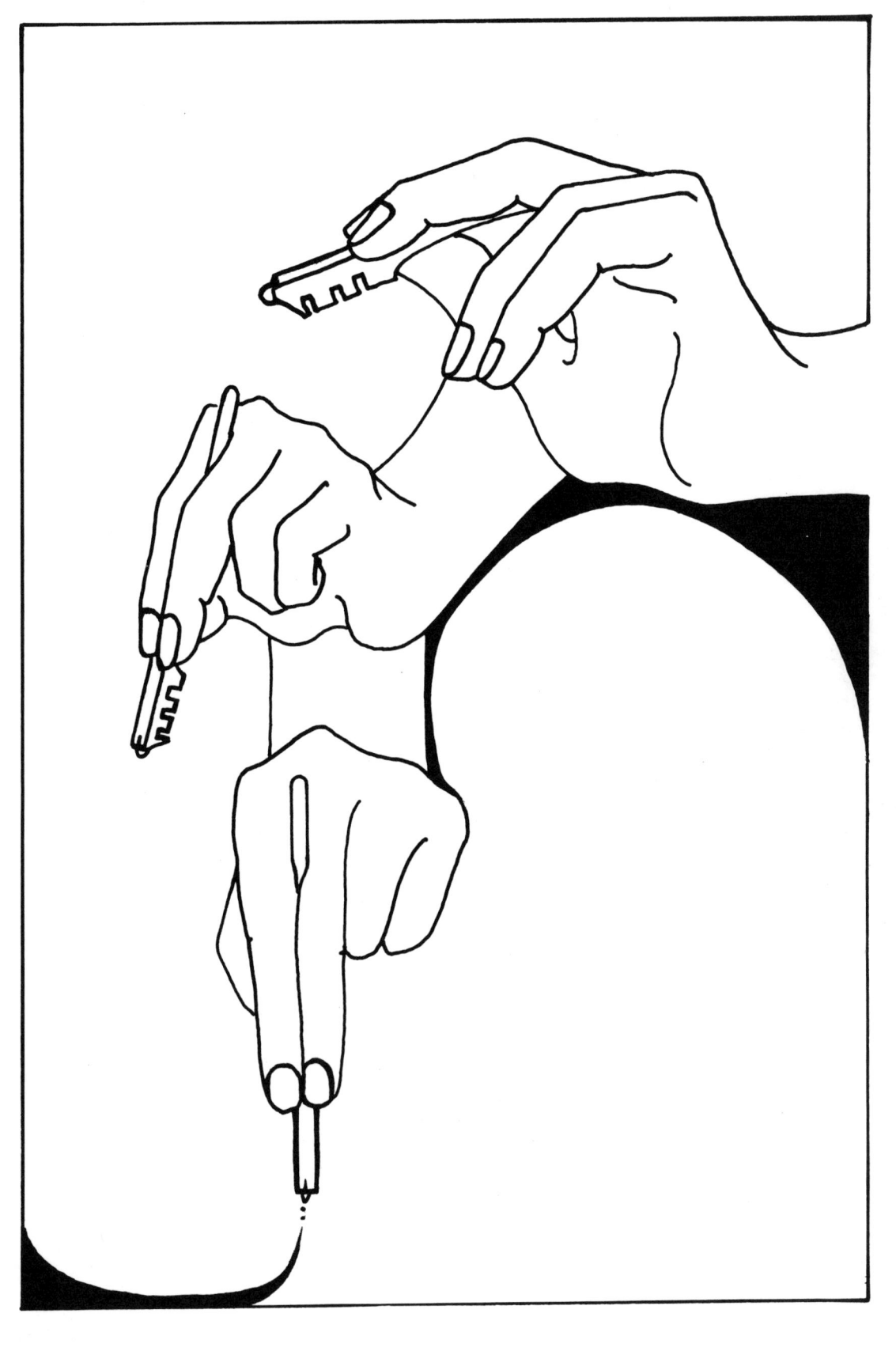

By standing over the glass you will have better leverage than when sitting. This position also permits the free movement of your cutting arm, while the other hand and arm are employed in holding the guide and glass steady. When using a cutting guide (straightedge, try square, etc.), the cutter must remain in tight contact with the guide's edge throughout the score.

Because the glass cutter does not cut but actually only scratches a line for the break to follow, it is important that the score line runs from edge to edge. This is accomplished by beginning and ending all score lines slightly off the edge of the glass.

Ill. 6-2

Scoring the glass from edge to edge.

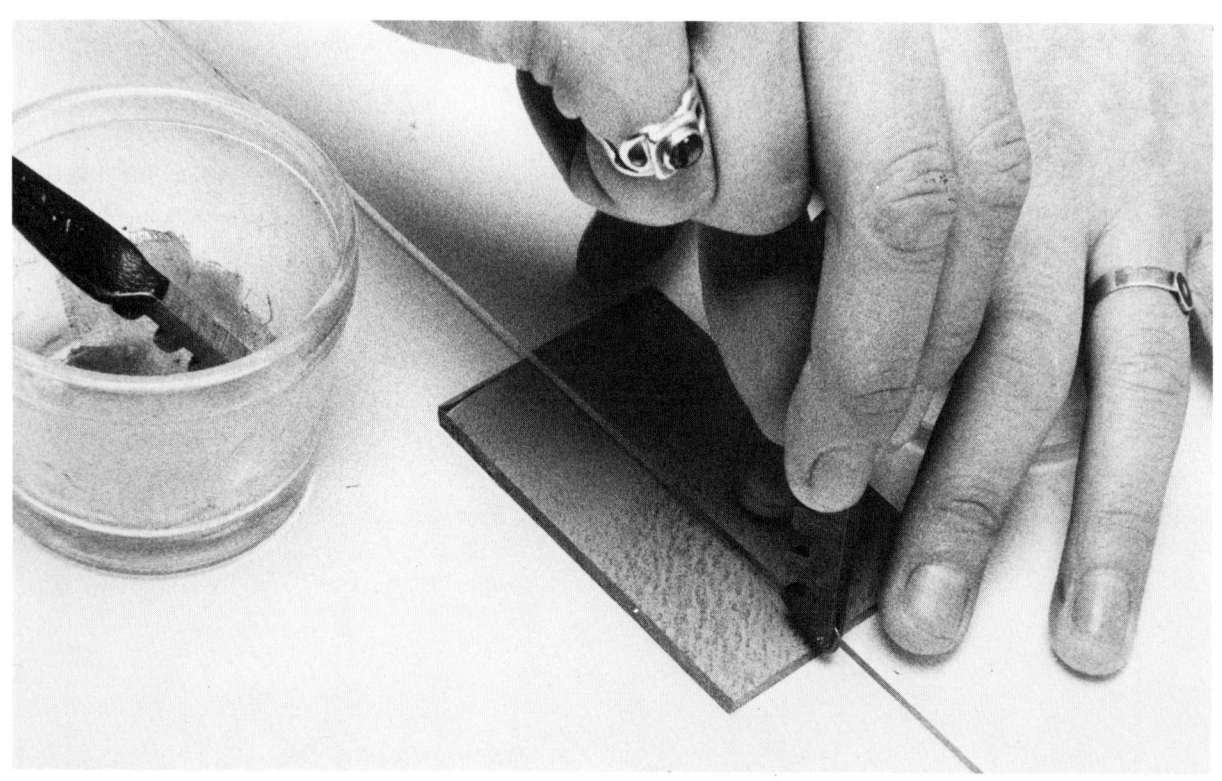

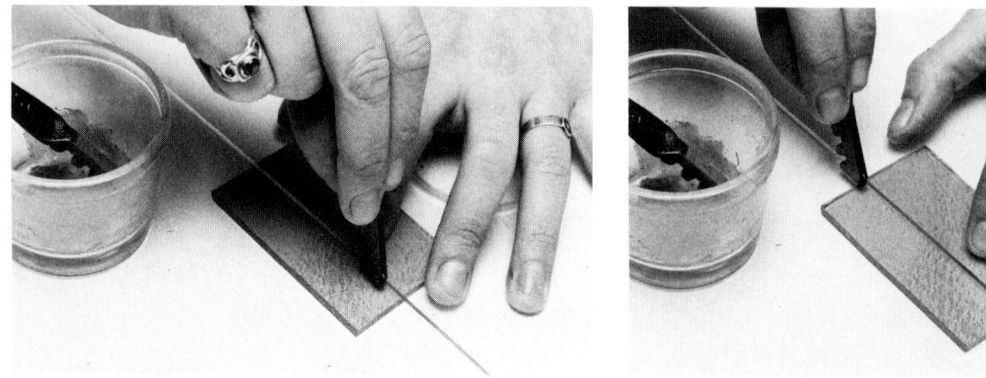

Breaking

While you will not always have to tap glass for it to break, it is important to know how this is done for those times when it is necessary. Hold the glass in one hand in a loose fist position in which the bottom edge is pressed between your thumb and index finger. In this position your fingers will be parallel and close to the score, providing support to the glass and acting as a guide for the tap (Ill. 6-3). Next, hold the glass cutter in your other hand, upside down and beneath the glass. Tap the score line with the ball of the cutter in a sharp, quick motion. This may take a bit of force, but when done correctly, it will cause a small fissure in the score line slightly above the bottom edge of the glass.

Whether you tap the glass or not, the actual breaking procedure is the same. Place your right hand to the right of the score line in a mirror image of your left hand. Simultaneously pull your thumbs apart and break upward. Never work a break back and forth; it is always the single motion that produces a safe, clean break (Ill. 6-4). When you use breaking pliers to remove a slender piece of glass that might chip if tapped and is too thin to be held comfortably, the break is much the same—a simultaneous pulling and breaking motion (Ill. 6-5). To prevent the glass from splintering as the pliers close down, you can cover the jaws of the pliers with a cloth. The cloth will shape around the glass as the pliers are brought to the score line.

A simple, straight line generally breaks without needing a tap, while strong, curving lines usually need some, if not complete, tapping to bring about a clean separation. Learning when to tap or to use breaking pliers will develop as you work with different kinds of glass. Meanwhile, if, after applying sufficient pressure to break glass, it does not break, then tap the score line. The same kind of guideline applies to the pliers: when you cannot get a good grip on the glass, try the breaking pliers. As you study and work, you will discover different methods of tapping and breaking glass, but whatever method you employ, always position the glass down and away from your body to avoid flying chips and splinters that result from the break. This does not mean that you should not watch the break—just keep the glass at a reasonable distance.

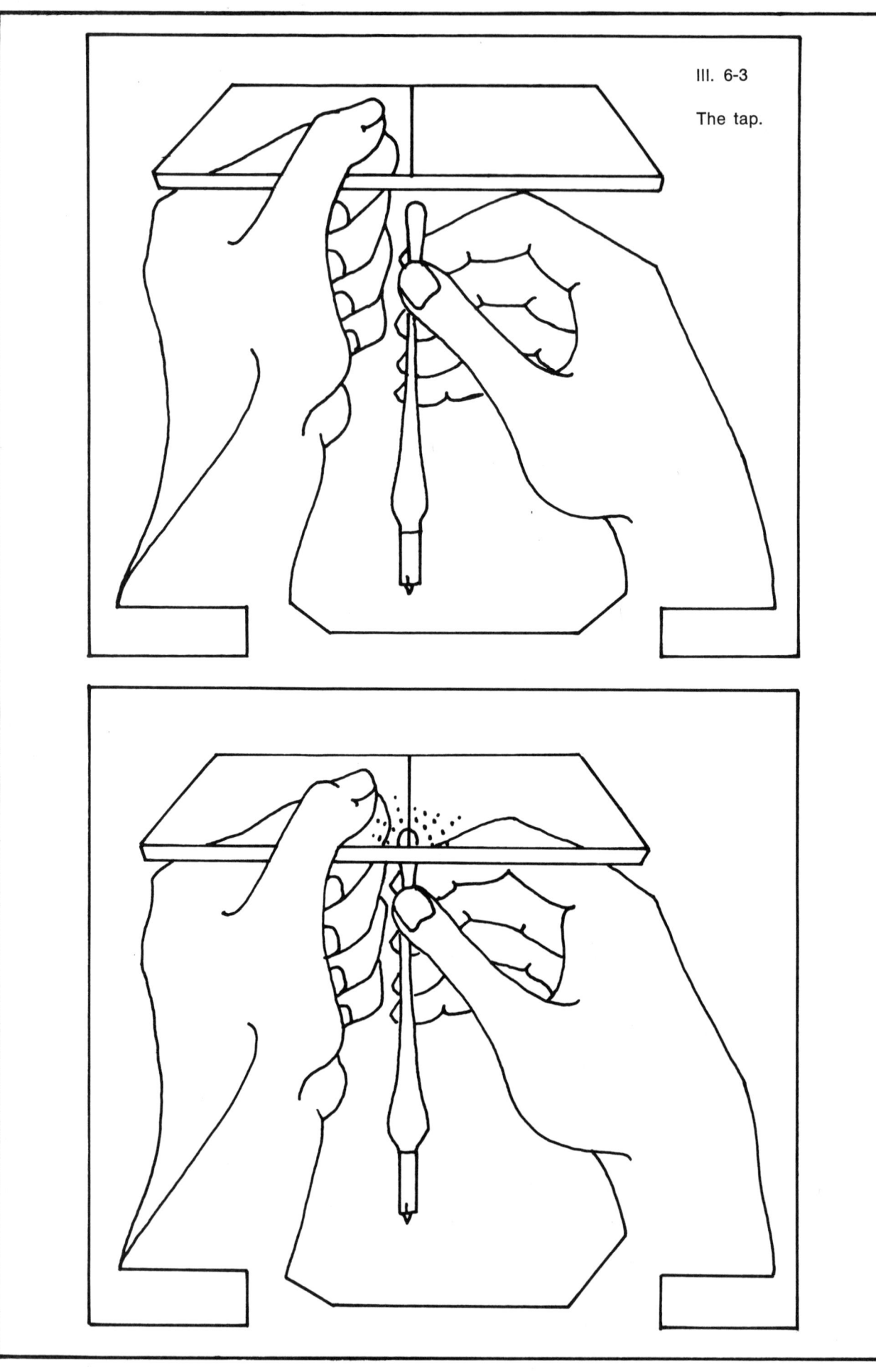

Ill. 6-3

The tap.

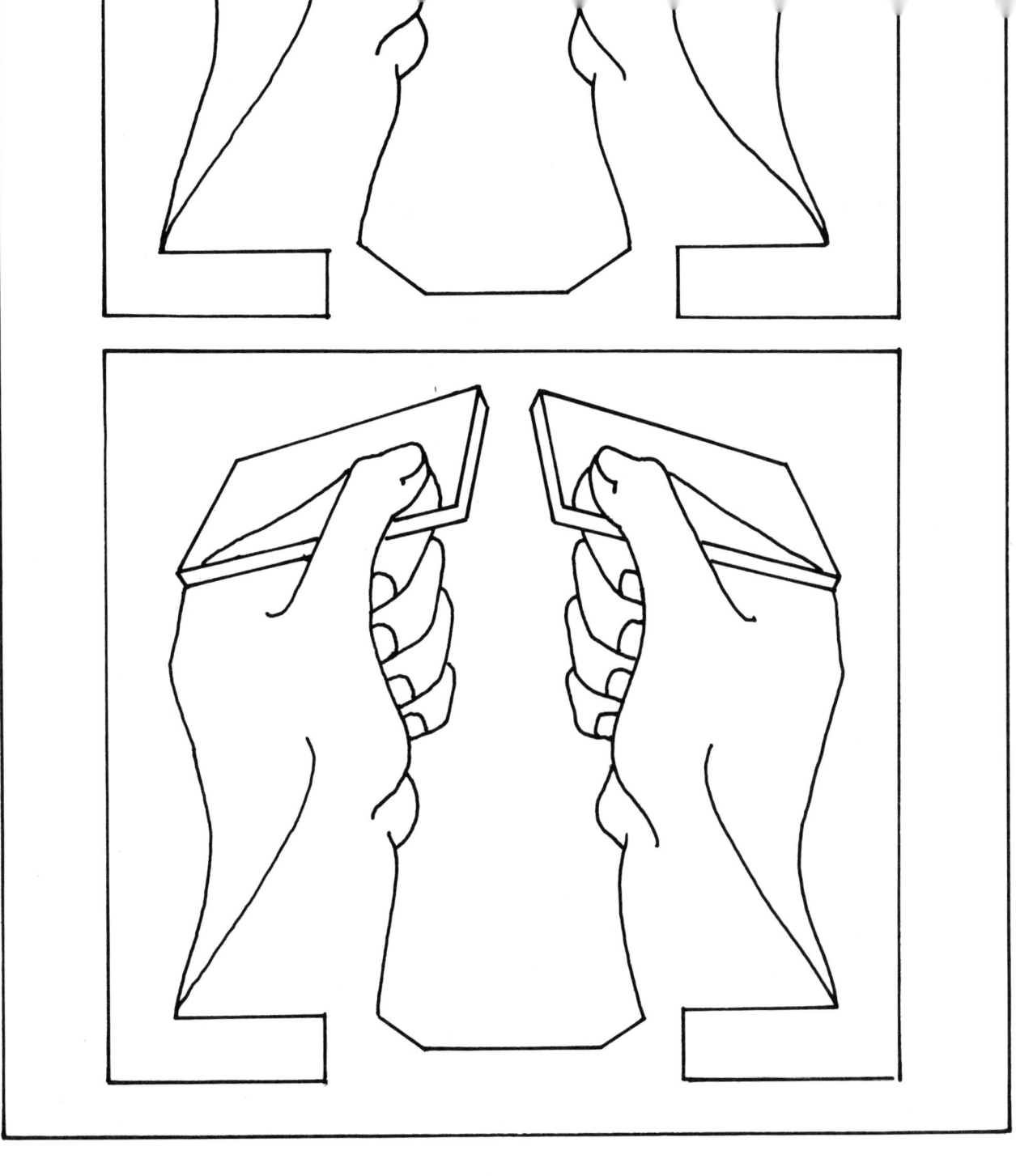

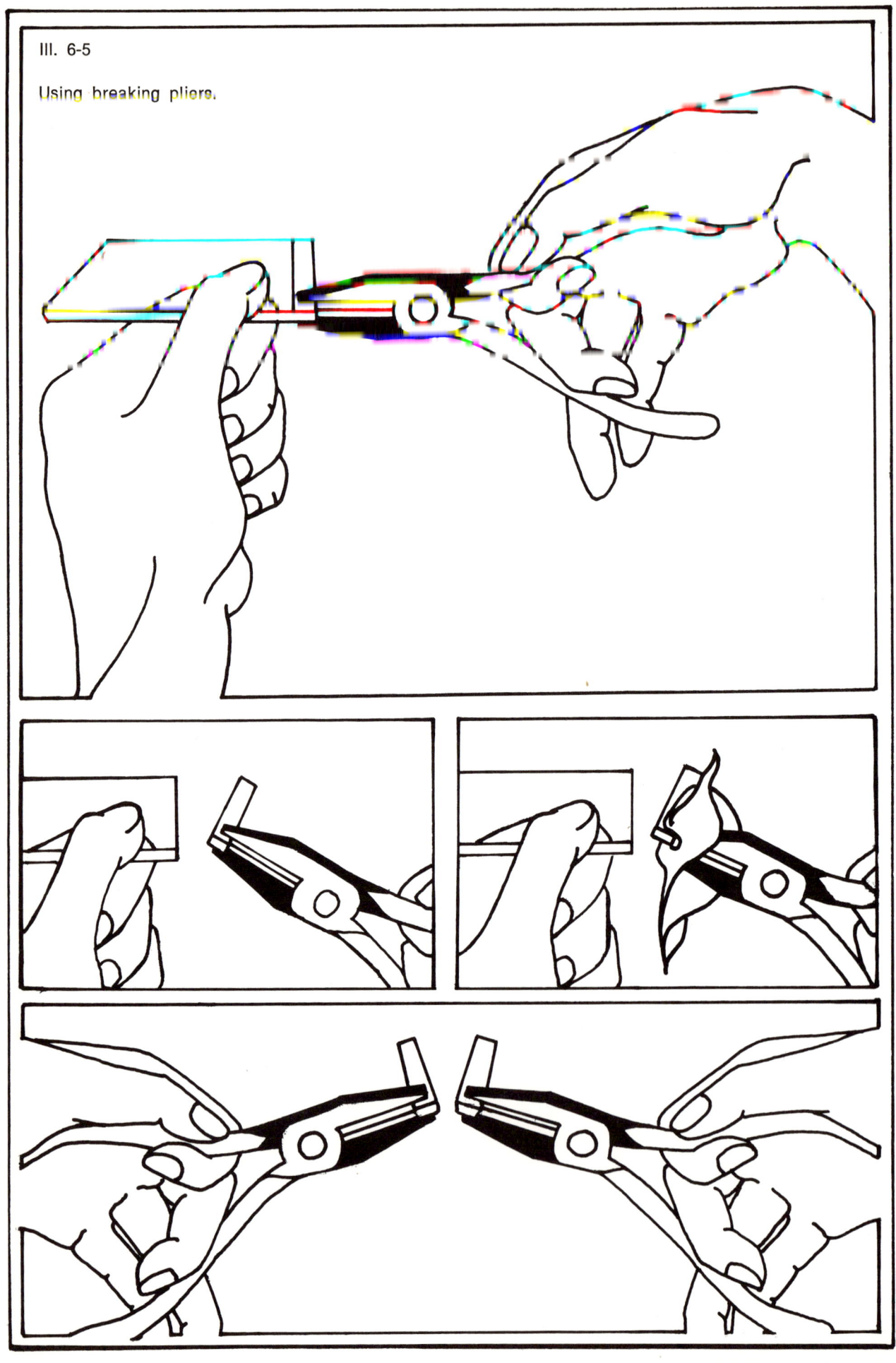

Ill. 6-5
Using breaking pliers.

Grozing and Wrapping

When you have cut all the glass pieces for a project, the next steps are to remove all discrepancies from the edges—a process called grozing—and to wrap the pieces in copperfoil. You will need the following tools:

grozing pliers and carbide sandpaper or grinding machine
copperfoil
razor blades
masking tape
metal straightedge

Cleaning up the edges of the glass you are about to wrap can be done with hand tools or by machine. Breaking pliers, grozing pliers, and carbide sandpaper are excellent hand tools that should be understood before setting up a grinding machine. Carefully examine the newly cut pieces for sharp edges and slivers that will protrude. These usually will be minuscule and transparent, but for the panel to fit together properly, they must be removed.

Hold the pliers in one hand and the glass in the other, and crush off these edges. As the jaws bite down, they tend to remove more than is wanted, so initially do not bite too far into the glass. If, after the pliers are used, the edges still need work, gently sand them down with carbide sandpaper. The finer the grozing work, the tighter the fit of the finished panel.

If you decide to purchase a grinding machine, follow these guidelines for its use. Hold the glass so that the edge to be grozed is pointing toward the floor. In this way the glass contacts the spinning wheel at a 45-degree angle. By doing both sides in this manner, the entire edge will be ground to a slight bevel. It is important to keep the glass moving across the spinning wheel so that it does not shatter due to excessive friction (heat) on any one spot. The wheel should be slightly lubricated with oil—not too much, or the excess will spin off onto your shoes when the machine is turned on. Before using any grozing method on glass cut specifically for a panel, experiment with any piece of scrap glass.

When the glass edges are smooth, they are ready for wrapping in copperfoil. You can buy copperfoil on rolls of precut widths, but it is more expensive and limited to a few widths and weights. Most glassworkers buy large rolls of foil that are six inches wide and cut their own strips. For most work the strips should measure slightly less than ¼ inch in width. (Don't bother measuring with a ruler; you can judge it by eye.) The more copperfoil is handled, the more difficult it becomes to work with; consequently, only cut off as much as you will use—generally a piece slightly less than two feet long. To keep the roll from becoming oxidized and crinkled, immediately tape down the cut edge to the roll and store it in a dry place.

Never cut foil over an uncovered wood surface, because the razor blade will tend to follow the wood grain rather than the direction you have in mind. Cover the surface with either a large piece of cardboard or a few sheets of newspaper taped securely to the work surface. The copperfoil is then cut over this protected surface (Ill. 6-6).

After cutting the strips, remove them from the board but keep the tape on one end. Hang the whole sheet by fixing the tape to a wall. When you need a strip, simply hold the tape at the top of the sheet and rip off a strip where it meets the tape. This method ensures as little crinkling of the foil as possible, and the individual strips are easier to remove.

As you cut the strips, make sure the motion produces a clean edge in a single cut. Two or three connecting cuts will weaken the strip, which may then tear while you are wrapping. All that is necessary for this single perfect cut is to have a straightedge that is longer than the length of foil you are cutting and sharp razor blades. The whole razor edge should be dragged through the foil—never use only the corner of the blade to make the cut. A mat knife will also work quite well.

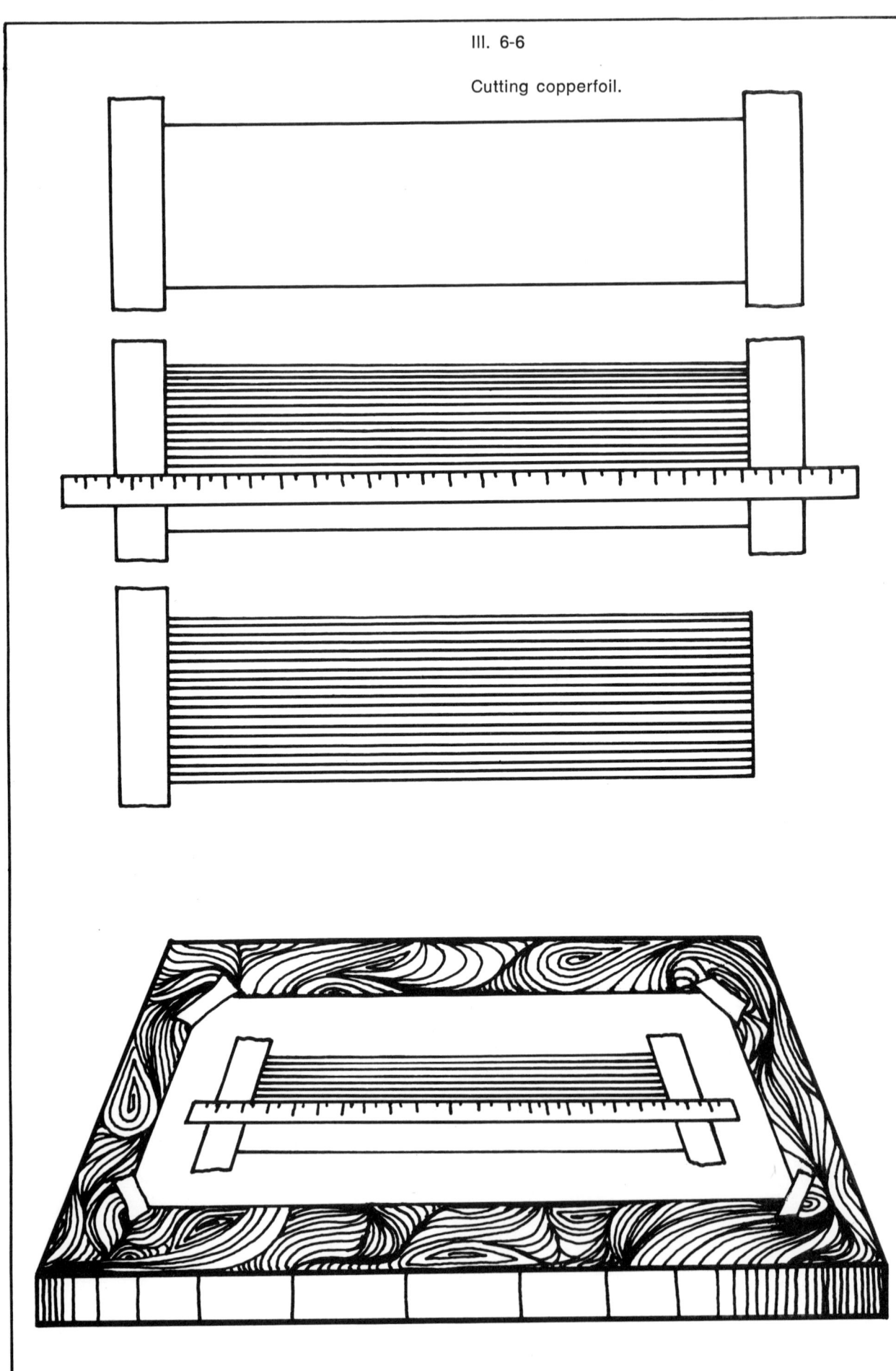

Ill. 6-6

Cutting copperfoil.

The most important thing to remember when wrapping a piece of glass is to keep the foil taut and crimped securely. As an aid to wrapping, you can spray one side of the individually cut strips with spray adhesive and allow it to become tacky before you wrap it against the edge of the glass. (The precut strips already have adhesive on them.) Hold the glass in one hand, the foil in the other. The one hand holds the foil in place on the glass edge, while the other guides and wraps the strip around the edge. The beginning ¼ inch or so of the strip is centered on the edge under a corner and held against the glass with your fourth finger. It is then wrapped around the immediate corner and held in place. Keeping constant pressure on this point, draw the foil around the remaining corners until it reaches and overlaps the starting point. Here it is sharply ripped off and held in place. A strip of foil will then surround the entire edge with an overhang of approximately 1/16 inch on either face of the glass. Crimp this overhang flat to the glass face, flattening a side first, then a corner, then another side, a corner, a side, etc. When you have finished crimping the copperfoil, it will form a channel in the shape of a U around the piece. (Another method is to crimp as you wrap around the edge.)

By sighting down the glass as you wrap it, you will be able to tell if the foil is moving off to one side or the other and to make an immediate correction. Do not try reusing any strips that become ripped or twisted while wrapping. Throw them out and use fresh foil. Since you cannot simply lay pieces of foil over each other and expect them to stay together, ripped strips must be removed and the whole piece of glass rewrapped in fresh foil. Also watch your beginning corners; if the foil was not centered properly and a section protrudes too far onto one face of the glass after the piece is wrapped, cut off the excess with a razor blade.

As each piece is wrapped, immediately place it in its proper position in the design and do not move it again. In this way a copper frame is gradually formed, ready for soldering. The neater and tighter you can wrap a piece, the better it will look after being covered with solder. (Note: one of the real hazards of this technique will not become noticeable until you have done a few panels. The strips of copperfoil tend to inflict small, barely noticeable cuts. As the hours pass, these cuts accumulate oil and dirt and start to be mildly irritating. At the end of a week they will be painful, and after a few months your fingers will become discolored and insensitive. Professional glassworkers avoid this problem with finger guards. To make these, wrap pieces of tissue paper around the fingers that you're using and cover to the first joint with masking tape.)

Ill. 6-7

Wrapping glass with copperfoil.

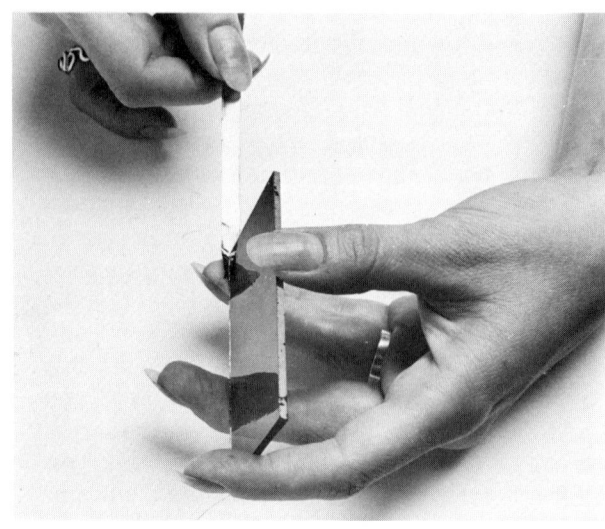
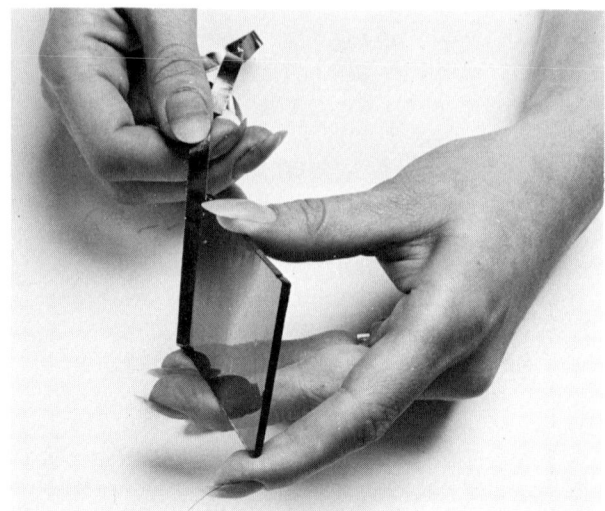

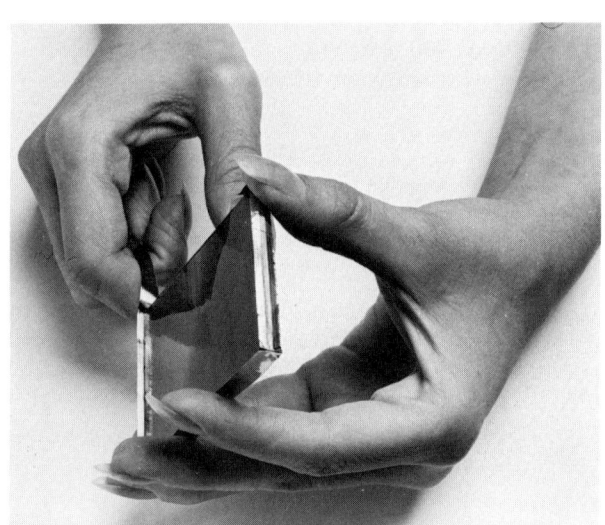

Ill. 6-8

Crimping the copperfoil to the glass and placing each wrapped and crimped piece in its proper place in the design.

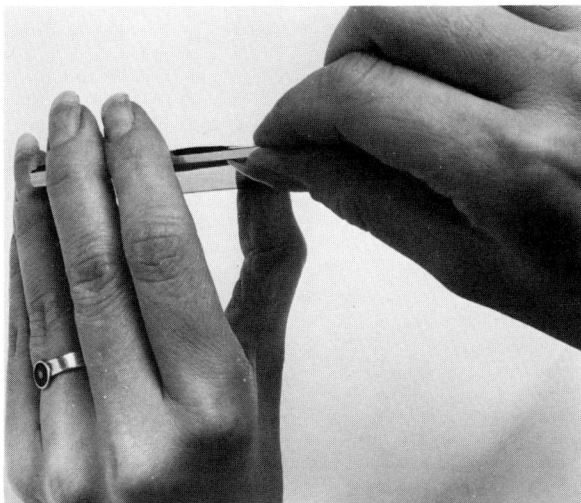
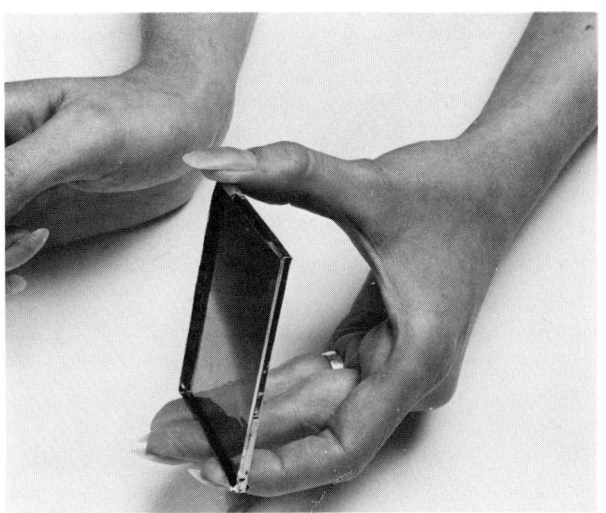

Soldering

When each piece of glass has been wrapped and placed over your transfer copy of the design, you are ready to solder. You will need the following tools:

hammer
horseshoe nails
¼-inch paintbrush
liquid flux
shallow container
solder
soldering iron
rasp or bastard file
tinning lid
brick or iron holder
cellulose sponge

There are three stages of soldering involved in glassworking: tacking, tinning, and beading, which are analogous to sewing's pinning, basting, and final stitching. Done once or twice, tacking and tinning are learned quickly and casually. The last stage, beading, is legitimately hard, however, and deserves every bit of your total concentration in mastering the technique. Think of the concentration that it took as a child to lace up your own shoes and how unconscious that action has become. By learning the pure mechanics of anything so that it becomes second nature, your freedom of choice is enhanced —and so it goes with glasswork.

Because you will be working with both hands at the same time—one hand holds the soldering iron while the other holds the roll of solder— you will be inclined to watch your hands— wrong! Watch the solder to see how it flows, heats, and cools.

Flux acts as a catalyst between solder and copperfoil, and it must be brushed onto the foil both before and during soldering in generous quantities. Without flux, solder will not even begin to stick to the copperfoil. The instant that flux (glycerine based) is brushed on, copperfoil begins to corrode (oxidize). At the same time, certain chemicals within the flux start evaporating. These reactions influence soldering. The evaporating chemicals leave behind a gummy residue that hampers the flow of the solder, and the oxidized foil, if left overnight, is very difficult to work with on the following day. To correct gumminess, wipe off the tip of your iron and reflux the line on which you are working. Oxidized foil is a bit more difficult to correct. It involves scraping the foil surface with the hot tip of your iron until the tip breaks through the oxidized part and reaches the untouched foil below. The foil is generally torn in this process, and the finished panel always shows that the foil was allowed to become oxidized. Since flux cannot be washed off the foil easily without causing even more damage, all soldering work should be completed within a day or two after you apply the flux.

If the iron becomes too hot, the solder will melt through the line to the opposite side of the panel; if too cold, the solder will lump and bunch together into a miniature mountain range. The exact temperature for the iron is learned through careful observation of the solder as it reacts to heat. To control the solder, your iron will have to be turned off every few minutes, allowed to cool for a few seconds, then turned on again. But work need not be stopped during these periods.

The above explanations pertain to all the stages of soldering. Now we will consider each of the stages in more detail.

Ill. 6-9

The stages of soldering: at top left, a panel wrapped in copperfoil resting against the lath strip on a work surface; at top right, the panel tacked together; at bottom left, the panel tinned; and at bottom right, the panel beaded. The circular detail shows a slice-away view of the unsoldered copperfoil line and the same line with a finished bead.

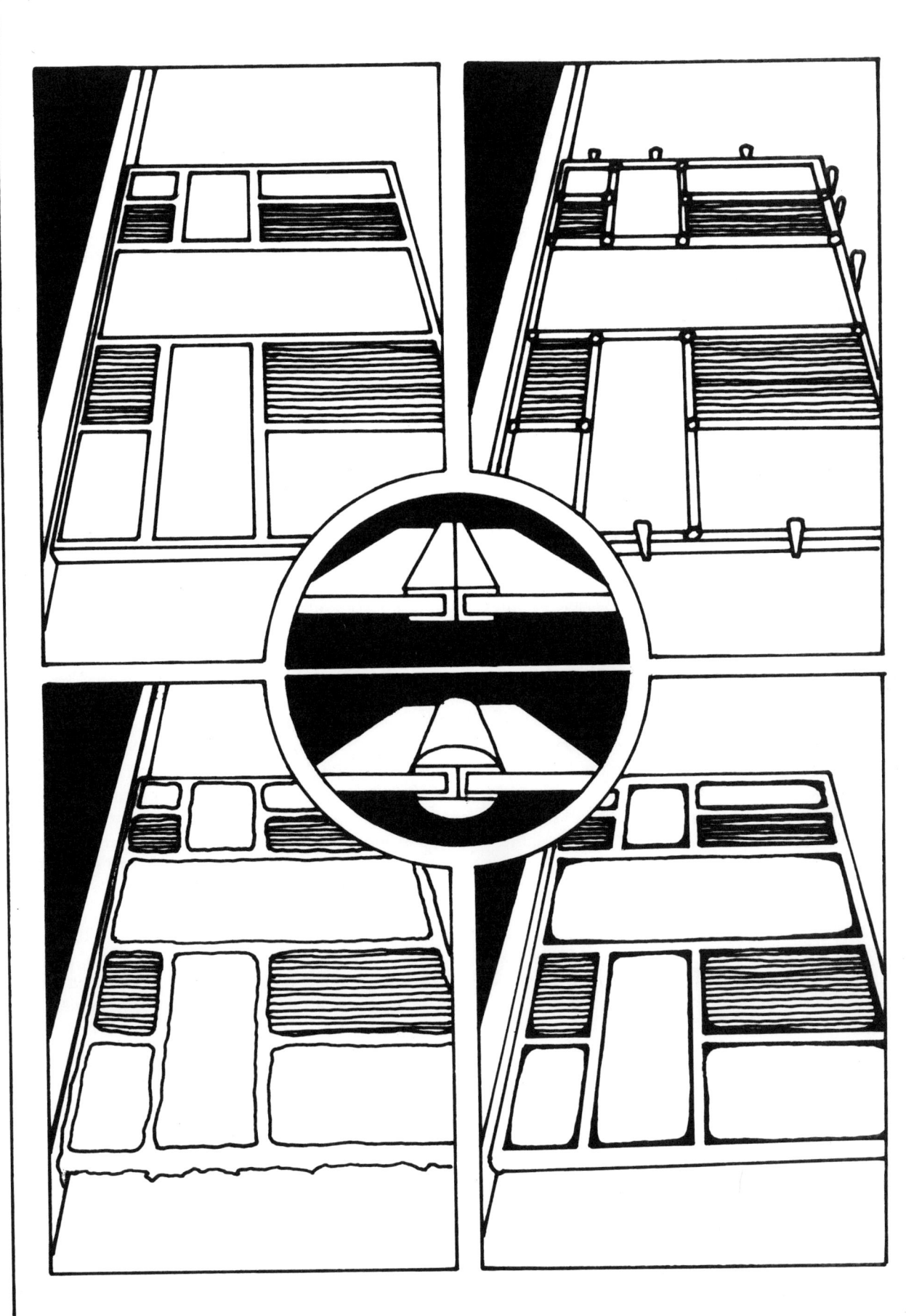

Tacking

When you have wrapped each piece of the glass in copperfoil and reassembled all of them against the lath strip on the work surface, secure the panel in place by surrounding it with a wall of support nails driven into the work surface. Now you can proceed to tack the panel together with drops of solder. Only one side of each panel needs to be tacked in order to hold it together. First brush flux onto the joints and then melt a large drop of solder over each joint. When all the joints are tacked together and the support nails have been removed, the panel is ready to be tinned. At this point, the panel is only loosely held together and should not be moved until this first side has been tinned and beaded.

Tinning

Tinning, in general, means covering a metal surface with a thin coat of tin. In the case of glassworking, copperfoil is coated with a solder composed of tin and lead. It should be noted that this is the same kind of tinning that takes place on the tip of your soldering iron, which is explained later in this chapter. Tinning the copperfoil serves a double purpose; not only are you preparing the foil surface to receive the finished bead, but you are also filling small gaps between the individually wrapped pieces of glass.

Brush a generous amount of flux over the entire visible foil structure, including the joints where drops of solder tack the panel together. Then, keeping the tip of your iron in constant contact with the extended wire of solder and the copperfoil, pull a thin coat of molten solder over the well-fluxed surface of the foil. A delicate touch is needed here, or your iron will tear and crumple the copperfoil or push the pieces of glass apart. The whole tinning process is greatly aided by the fact that 60/40 solder heats and cools almost instantaneously and, in its liquid state, tends to "run" a line of its own accord.

Beading

The bead is the finished lead surface in a smooth, high, rounded shape. It is this specific shape that gives a panel strength, durability, and, through its manipulation, an increased beauty in the design. The tinned copperfoil of the panel must now be thought of in terms of a pattern—long horizontal and vertical lines that run from edge to edge, intersecting at points and stopping at the perimeter. Perimeter soldering work has its own peculiarities and is explained later on.

The bead is laid down, drop by connecting drop, with the first drop cooling as the second drop connects with it. In this way you form a high, rounded shape as you move down the line. Bead all the lines of one direction (either vertical or horizontal), then turn the panel so that the unfinished lines will run in the same direction, and bead them up to the point of intersecting the previously beaded lines. Generally, you connect intersecting lines with an additional drop of solder; do not try to pull the solder from either side with the heated iron.

When the first side is fully beaded, turn the panel over, and tin and bead the other side in the same manner. The panel will be ready for perimeter soldering only after both sides of the panel have been completely soldered.

Quite often you will have to rework the bead a few times, because of the general ugliness of the line. A finished bead should have a smooth, unmarred surface that dips and rises in a gradual, graceful way. But the height and roundness of the bead should never be sacrificed for a mere smoothness of the line. To rework the bead, start from an outside edge and work toward the opposite edge. This action is similar to that of laying the original bead, but it is done mostly with the heat of the iron, adding solder only in very small quantities. Lower and raise the tip of the iron in and out of the bead so that the hot tip repeatedly presses through the bead and touches the copperfoil before it is raised again. As you press the tip into the bead, fingers of heat will travel in front of the tip, and this area will also begin to melt. Quickly raise the tip and place it directly into the semimelted area—thus smoothing the line by connecting areas of heat with an up-and-down motion. *Never drag the tip through the bead, or you will sacrifice the entire line in doing so.* You will probably need another drop or two of solder each time you reach an intersection.

As your hands become accustomed to holding the iron and solder (both will seem heavy at first) and as your eyes adjust to watching the solder flow, the work will cease to be difficult. Save your first practice panel to boost your morale by the time you complete your fifth panel. The quality difference will be quite amazing, while the length of time required to complete this later work will be less than half the time you spent on your first endeavor. In summary, the secrets of building a fine, high line are:

(1) use a lot of solder and flux,
(2) watch how the solder is affected by heat,
(3) keep your iron clean and well tinned,
(4) watch the iron's heating and cooling.

Ill. 6-10

Laying the finished bead over the tinned surface.

Ill. 6-11

Reworking a poorly beaded line.

Perimeter Soldering

Because the perimeter of a panel is a three-dimensional surface with two sides and a top, it is more difficult to solder than the flat lines on either face of a panel. Each time you solder a perimeter, you are engaging in a battle with gravity. Most copperfoil workers give up too easily and are left with a weak perimeter that tears and falls apart. If you work slowly with a fairly cool iron and use solder in smaller amounts, some of these difficulties will be avoided. Also, make sure that the pieces of glass that form the perimeter are wrapped in foil slightly wider than ¼ inch, thus increasing your soldering surface and aiding soldering work.

Ill. 6-12

The three stages of perimeter soldering: the unsoldered perimeter, the partially beaded perimeter, and the completely beaded perimeter.

To solder the perimeter, first flux and bead both sides of the perimeter. Then prop the panel on its edge so that it stands perpendicular to the work surface and lay a bead on top of the two side beads. With this three-stage method, you place just the exact amount of solder on the perimeter's edge so that it can be held without overflowing. If the solder rolls off the top, your panel is not perpendicular but leaning toward one side. When this happens, solder drops will streak down the face of the panel and cover previously beaded lines and the glass. To help prevent drips from sticking to the previously soldered lines, wipe off excess flux from these lines before beginning perimeter work. If the drip sticks, you have to rework the damaged lines.

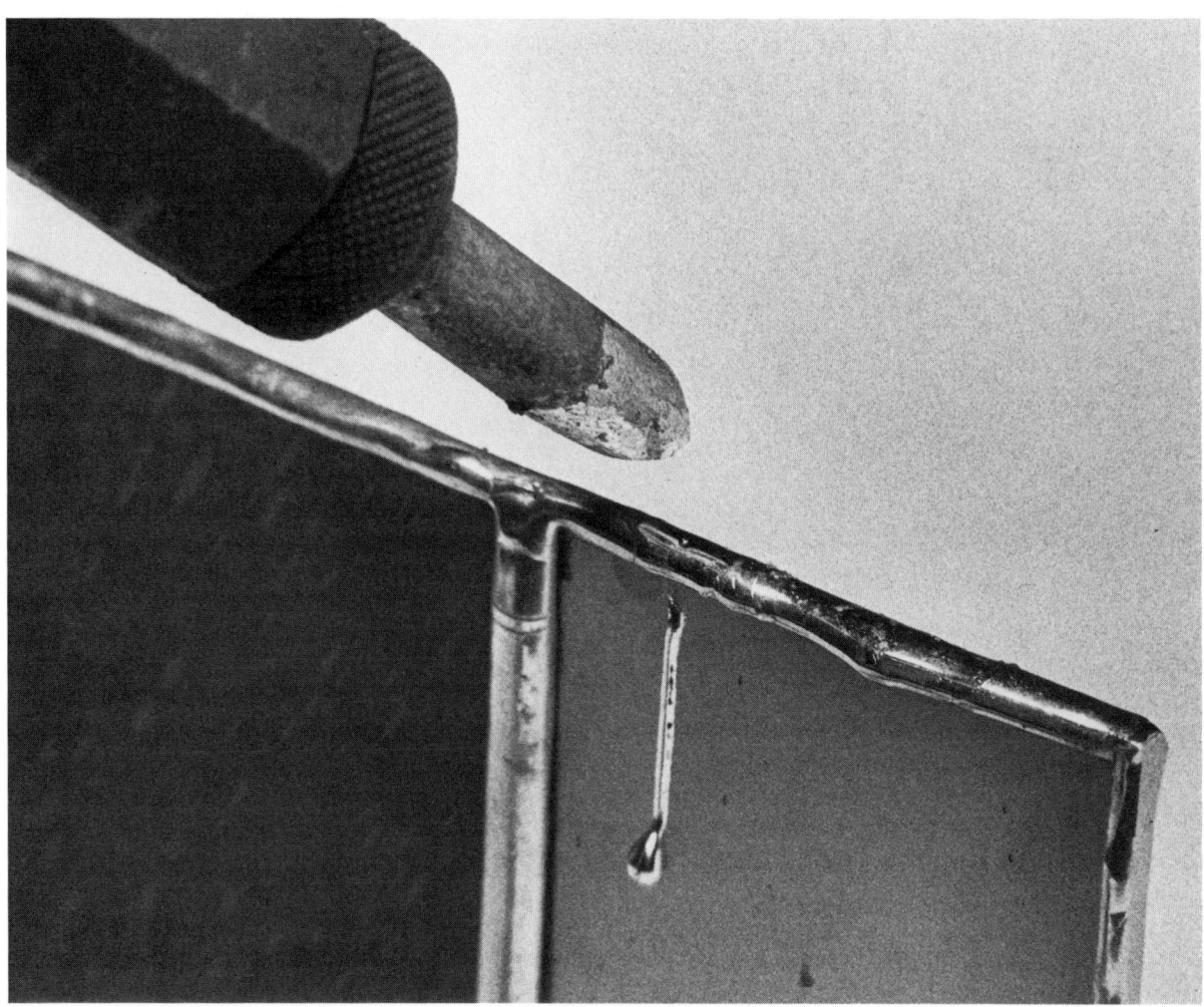

Ill. 6-13

A panel propped into position for laying the finished bead on the perimeter; the drip of solder is a common occurrence.

Hanging Loops

When the perimeter is finished, scrub the panel clean in hot, soapy water with a little ammonia added. Dry it and add hanging loops (Ill. 6-14). Unless you have designed the panel specifically to turn and spin in the wind, each panel will require two hanging loops. These can be made from either copper wire or paper clips that are bent to a circular or *omega* shape. Attach the loops one at a time in this way: after dipping the loop into flux, hold it with needle-nose pliers over the spot on the perimeter to which it will be attached. Make sure the panel is propped up perpendicular to the work surface. Using a hot iron and a drop of solder, melt the loop *into* the perimeter.

Of course, you may not always want to hang your panels. You can also display them on miniature easels, which you can bend from wire coat hangers. You can also buy small easels in art-supply stores.

Repair Work

It is almost never worth the effort to replace a piece of glass once a panel has been completely soldered. By the time you have repaired a six-square-inch panel, you almost could have duplicated the entire panel. However, for those times that the effort can be justified, here is how it is done. Hold the panel above the work surface in a flat, parallel position, and—working from the underside—melt the bead that surrounds the broken piece. Turn the panel over and melt the bead on the other side. The piece of glass will begin to fall away from the pieces surrounding it. Once the glass is free, run the iron around the empty space to remove as much solder as possible. Next, cut a replacement piece, wrap it in foil, lay it in place, and rebead the lines. Usually all the lines that connect with the repair area will have to be reworked—on both faces of the panel. This presents a further problem, because it is very difficult to rework a bead that is even a few days old. Since cracked pieces of glass in panels are almost unavoidable at some point and repair work is generally distasteful and boring, it might be a good idea to cultivate a cheerful, fatalistic philosophy toward cracked glass.

Reinforcement

Good copperfoil work results in a finished product that, if nothing else, is solid. Once joined, the individual pieces of glass should act as a single structure. If this is not the case, then the work (panel, lamp, etc.) needs reinforcement.

A basic method of reinforcement is to solder metal pieces onto, around, or over the weak area. You can approach this kind of work in a very natural way—adding reinforcement wherever it seems necessary. Many different shapes and kinds of metal can be used—brass strips, copper wire, hammered copper strips, pieces of lead came, paper clips, etc. If the metal will hold flux and solder, it can be used. Whether the area to be strengthened has a finished bead or has only been tinned, lay the piece of metal over the area and apply heat, flux, and solder until the metal is covered. If the reinforcing piece of metal spans an open space, make sure that it is well anchored at the points of connection. In either case you can make the support a hidden or a decorative addition to the piece itself.

You will probably have to spend very little time on this kind of reinforcing work, as long as you keep the pull of gravity in mind, work with small pieces of glass, avoid lines that bisect the design, and take care to solder high, rounded, beaded lines.

Ill. 6-14

Attaching omega-shaped hanging loops to the perimeter.

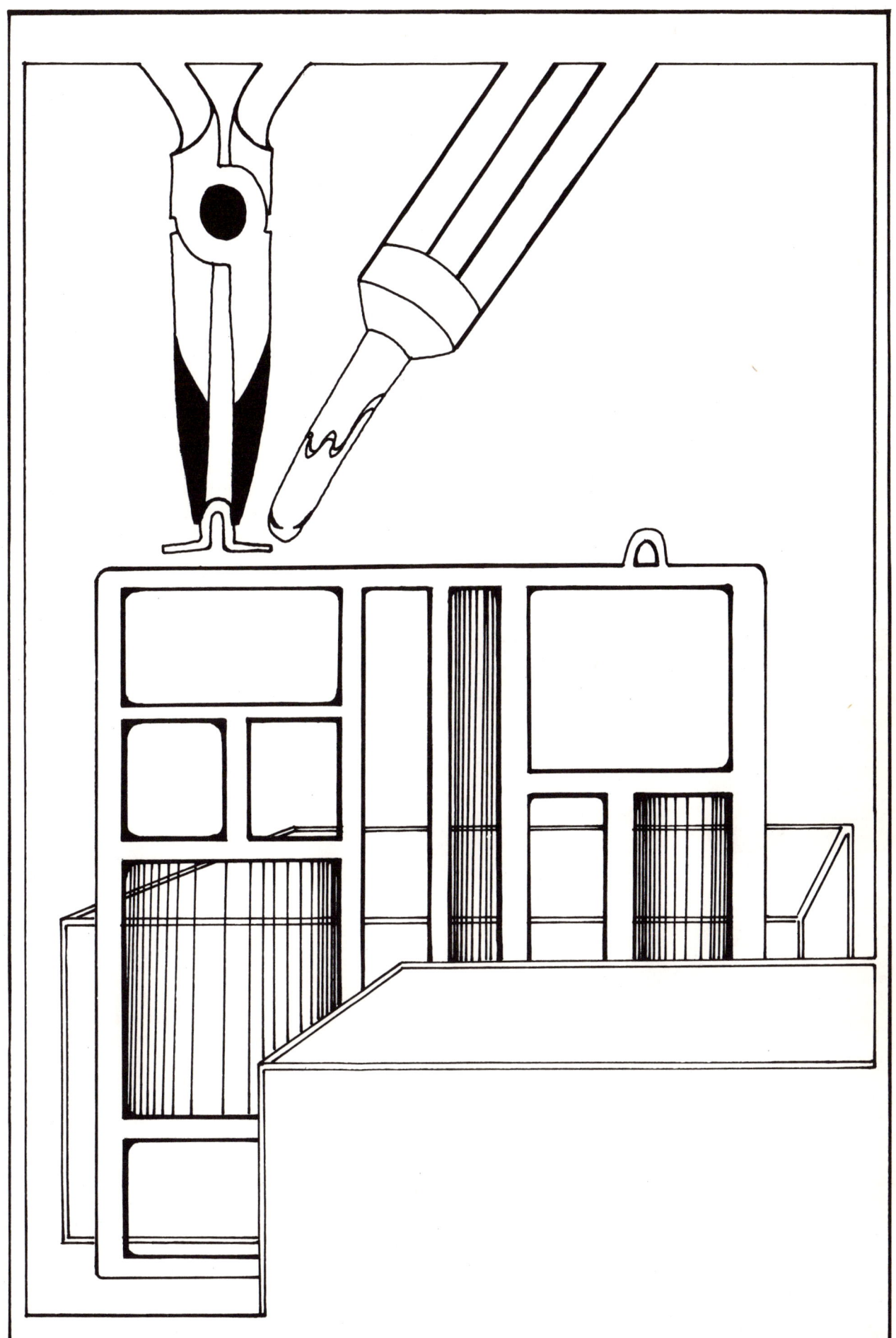

Cleaning and Tinning the Soldering Iron

Your soldering iron must always be freshly cleaned and tinned before you begin soldering work, or your craft level will suffer, the job of soldering will be more difficult, and it will take longer to accomplish. Both copper and iron-coated tips should be cleaned and tinned; iron-coated tips should not be filed until they become damaged (except for the Durotherm tip, which should never be cleaned by filing).

With the iron assembled and *cold,* file the tip with a rasp or bastard file to a bright copper shine. This is done by filing across and down the length of the tip with a gentle, rounding motion. Filing in this way will ensure a smooth, rounded shape and remove any pits or encrusted solder that will inhibit heat control. Always shape the end of the tip so that it will cover the maximum contact area between tip and work. This allows for the greatest transfer of heat.

Ill. 6-15

A newly cleaned tip of a soldering iron and the tip in the process of being tinned in a tinning lid.

Tinning—coating the *hot* tip with a thin deposit of solder—is always done immediately after cleaning. Allow the iron to heat for a few minutes while it is resting on a brick or in a special iron holder. Then pick up the iron in one hand and the tinning lid (see Chapter 3) in the other. (When the iron has reached the correct temperature for tinning, it will immediately melt the strip of solder into the tinning lid and sputter as it comes in contact with the flux.) Press the tip against the solder strip and manipulate the lid so that flux and solder coat the tip. When done correctly, the tip will shine like a mirror. If it does not shine, quickly wipe the tip, file the end, and try again. The main factors for this operation are: sufficient flux, solder, and speed. Another tinning method is to brush flux onto the hot tip and touch the solder to it, and then spread the molten solder with the brush.

While you are soldering, remember to wipe the hot tip with a cellulose sponge to keep it in good working shape. If, after two to four hours, the iron becomes extremely sluggish, allow it to cool, and then file the tip clean and retin it. This will make an extraordinary difference when you return to work.

Ill. 6-16

Three diverse and unusual ways of using the copperfoil technique. Gilly, true to his unique approach to glassworking, pushed the limits of copperfoil in each of them. The large pieces of glass in the architectural model normally would have demanded the use of lead came, but Gilly did it in copperfoil. The metal lamp is made entirely of solder and jewels wrapped in copperfoil, without the aid of the supporting superstructure that such a shape ordinarily would need. The plain-glass globe resulted from two accidents. When it was first dropped, Gilly repaired the breaks with copperfoil and beading (a delicate job in itself). When it was dropped a second time, Gilly filled the small hole with a whimsical jeweled bug.

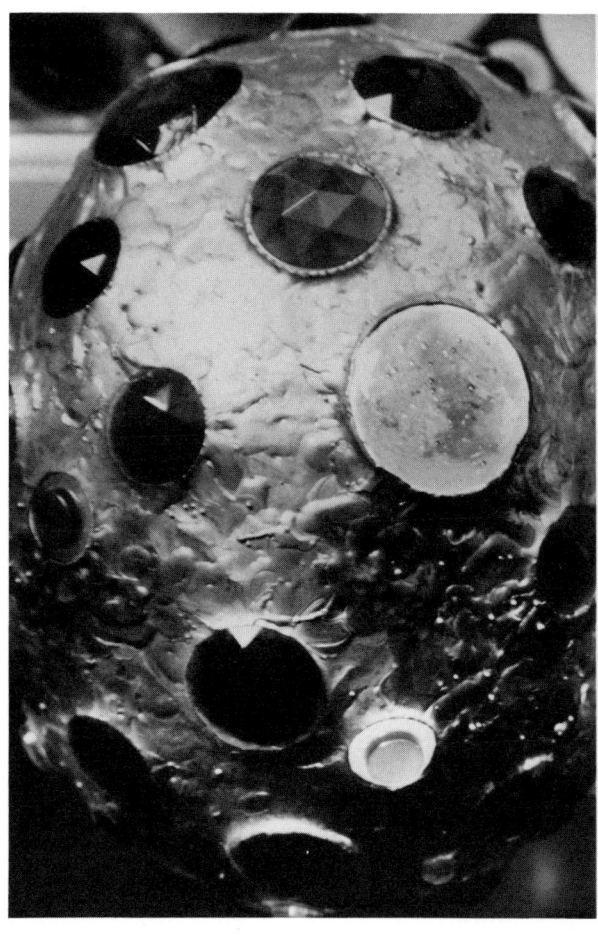
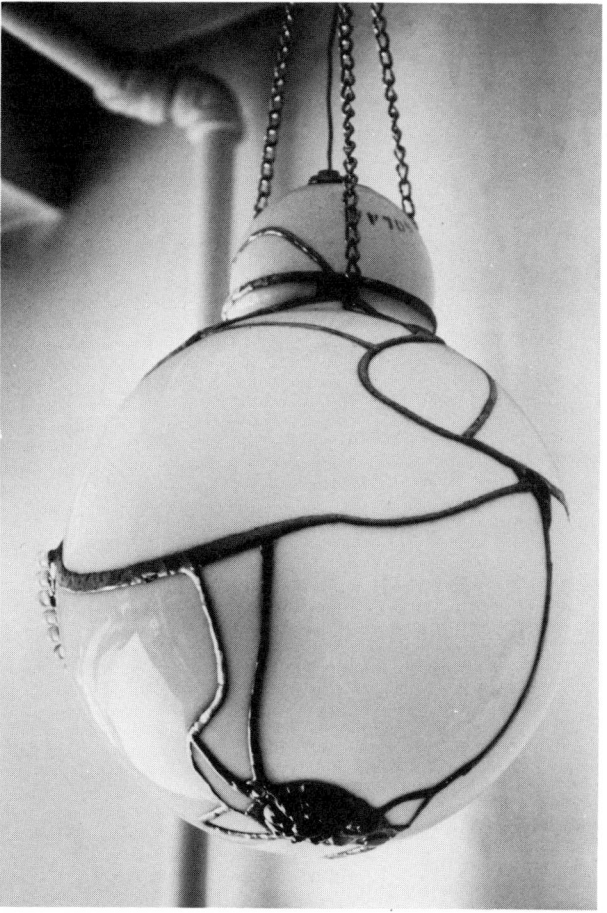

Chapter 7:

FIRST WORKS

It is great to see what others have done after a few years of practice, but it is even more important to get an idea of what you can accomplish in the first day of work. With this in mind, I photographed a friend while she was learning the technique. I specifically chose a nine-year-old without previous art training in an attempt to compensate for the fact that she was learning from a person rather than from a book. However, I did teach her exactly as I would teach an adult, and, with the exception of her soldering work (which was slightly above normal), the results were virtually the same.

Ills. 7-1 to 7-4

Nine-year-old Lori at work on her first panel: using breaking pliers, wrapping a small piece of glass from a continuous roll of adhesive-backed copper-foil, and laying the finished bead on the tinned panel. Finally, the finished panel, which is surprisingly strong and well soldered.

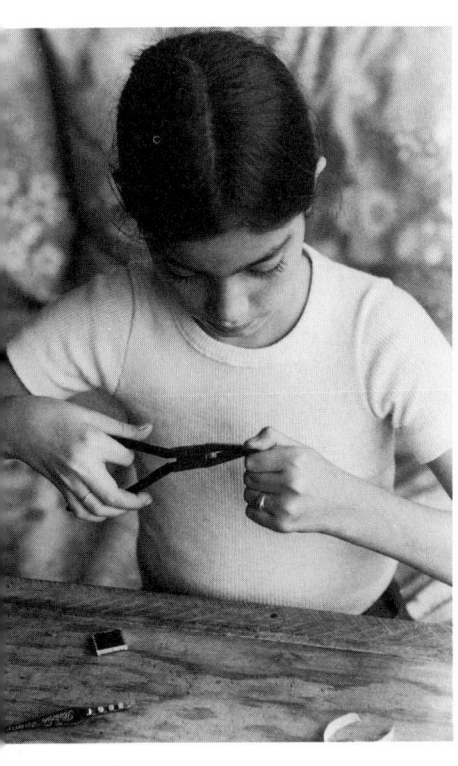 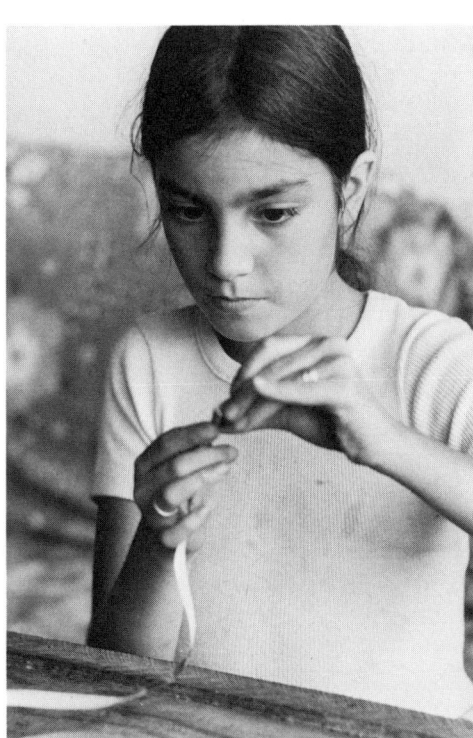 

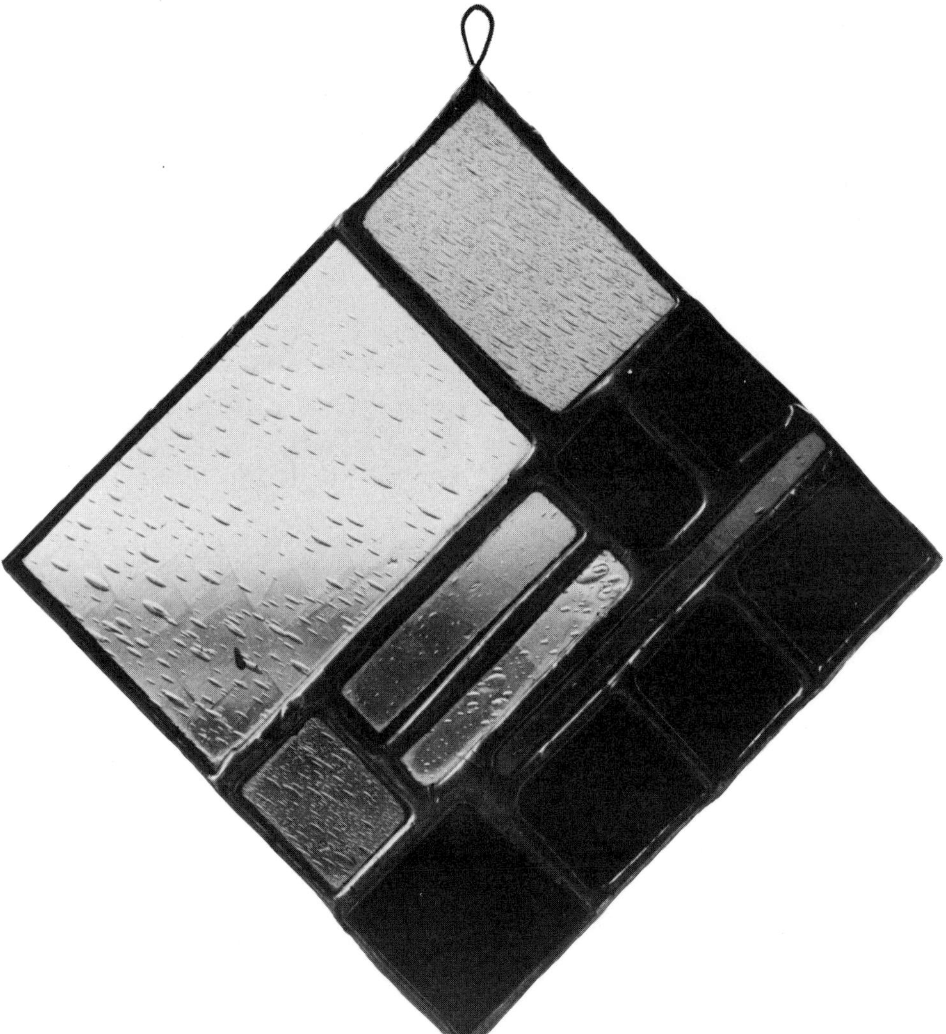

It took Lori approximately six hours to finish one five-inch square panel; three hours were spent becoming familiar with everything connected with cutting and breaking glass; wrapping was mastered within a few minutes; and the rest of the time was spent on soldering work. If Lori were to complete a similar panel each day for one week, her time by the end of the week would be down to about one hour for each panel, and her craft level would have risen considerably.

Ills. 7-5 to 7-9

All of these panels are typical practice panels, and in that sense they are first works. All measure about six inches square. Each was an experiment with different kinds of glass, heavy and light weights of copperfoil, new flux, or a new soldering iron.

By way of further reference I have included a few pieces of my own work and work from my friends. They do not necessarily represent the first few hours of work, but they are, nonetheless, first experiments.

Ills. 7-10 to 7-12

Two panels made by the author after six months of glassworking (the close-up view is a detail of the second panel). Both were made to test the strength of the copperfoil technique when working in large dimensions—and both remain solid to this day.

It is important to understand that although you may be quite adept at flat work (panels), the minute you begin to work with three dimensions, you return to the status of beginner. The same applies to the change from straight cuts to freehand curves. Everyone begins somewhere, and it is always awful; you forget to hold the cutter correctly or to check which side is the easiest to cut, and you make four or five terrible cuts before you realize that your problem was just that small detail. When you encounter a difficulty, run through a mental checklist or reread the section where that action is described. Also, whenever you begin a new phase —three dimensions, curves, mixed-media, or whatever—work simply. For example, make a box before you begin a lamp, and study the new problems of construction before beginning a more ambitious plan. After all, if a nine-year-old can do it. . . .

Ill. 7-13

A collection of early works—including Christmas-tree ornaments in the box.

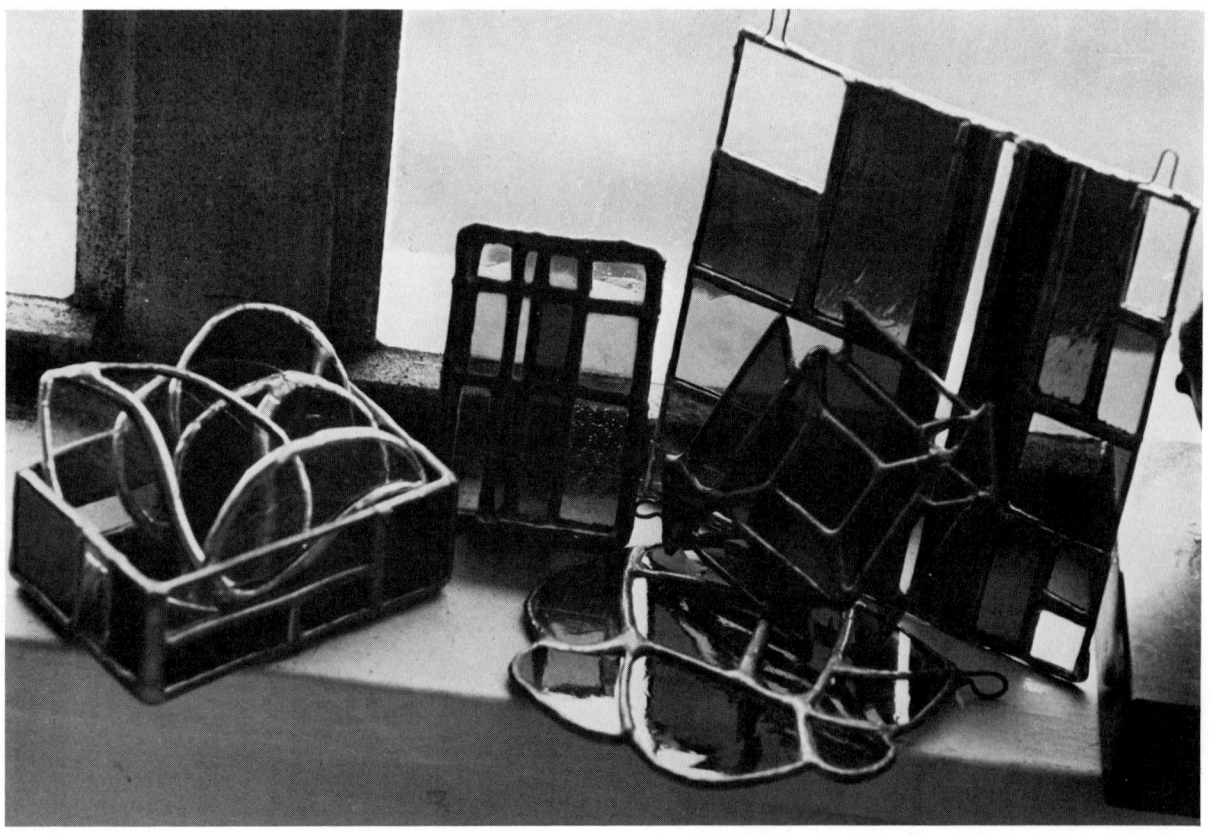

Ill. 7-14

Three hanging planters flank a small seven-sided box *(right)*, which was Lori's fifth project. Such boxes and planters are preludes to lamp making.

Chapter 8:

SPECIAL PROBLEMS

The Curve

You will be cutting curves for a long time before they will match the perfection of your straight-line cuts. The major stumbling blocks to working with curved lines are: scoring a smooth, continuous line; breaking a curve without losing a part of it (or destroying the whole piece); cutting two curves that fit tightly together when placed edge to edge; and knowing which shapes can and cannot be cut in glass. The solutions to these problems depend upon your knowledge and use of special cutting guides and your developing an intuitive feeling for the limits of glass.

Freehand Curves

Excluding the perfect circle (which requires a special tool), curves are basically either *C*- or *S*-shaped. The farther away from a straight line that a curve travels, the more difficult it becomes to cut and break. Therefore, *S* shapes are more difficult to achieve in glass than *C* shapes.

Before you cut a curved piece from a sheet of glass, remove a rectangle that measures slightly larger than the desired piece and then cut the curved piece from that. This will save a good deal of glass that would otherwise be ruined if the break ran wild.

While you are cutting, not only do your hand and arm act as one unit, but your whole body duplicates the motion of cutting. This movement, which at first is robotlike, soon becomes fluid and natural. When dealing with a deeply curving line, make a series of small scores rather than attempting to make a line in a single cut. The first few scores can be gently curving cuts, but, as you work into the curve, shorten your scores and increase their number. Break the scores in sequence. When you cut an outside curve, make a series of scores that follow the curving line and then run off the glass edge at a tangent to the curve. Also, break these out in sequence.

Because of the tensions and stresses that exist within a sheet of glass, most curves will require full or partial tapping to separate. This can be done in several ways: beginning at the top at one edge and working to the opposite edge, tapping at both edges and meeting in the middle, or tapping at the middle and working to the edges. Curves also can be broken with a tap-pull method that gradually moves the break along the score line to completion. Usually the score and the kind of glass will tend to dictate which method works best, but it is generally a good idea to cut and break inside curves before you cut and break outside curves. Another solution—one that works especially well for shallow curves—is to crush out the curve with a pair of grozing pliers.

Cutting Guides

Often, in order to cut a specific piece (or pieces), you will need the aid of a cutting guide. The artist Giotto won a large commission from Pope Benedict IX on the strength of his ability to paint a perfect circle—freehand. This is a simple feat compared to cutting a perfect circle from glass freehand. The *lens or circle cutter* is a tool that scores a perfect circle. It is available either mounted on a board or with a suction cup; the former type is preferable.

Ill. 8-1

The process of cutting perfect circles and arcs with the aid of a lens or circle cutter.

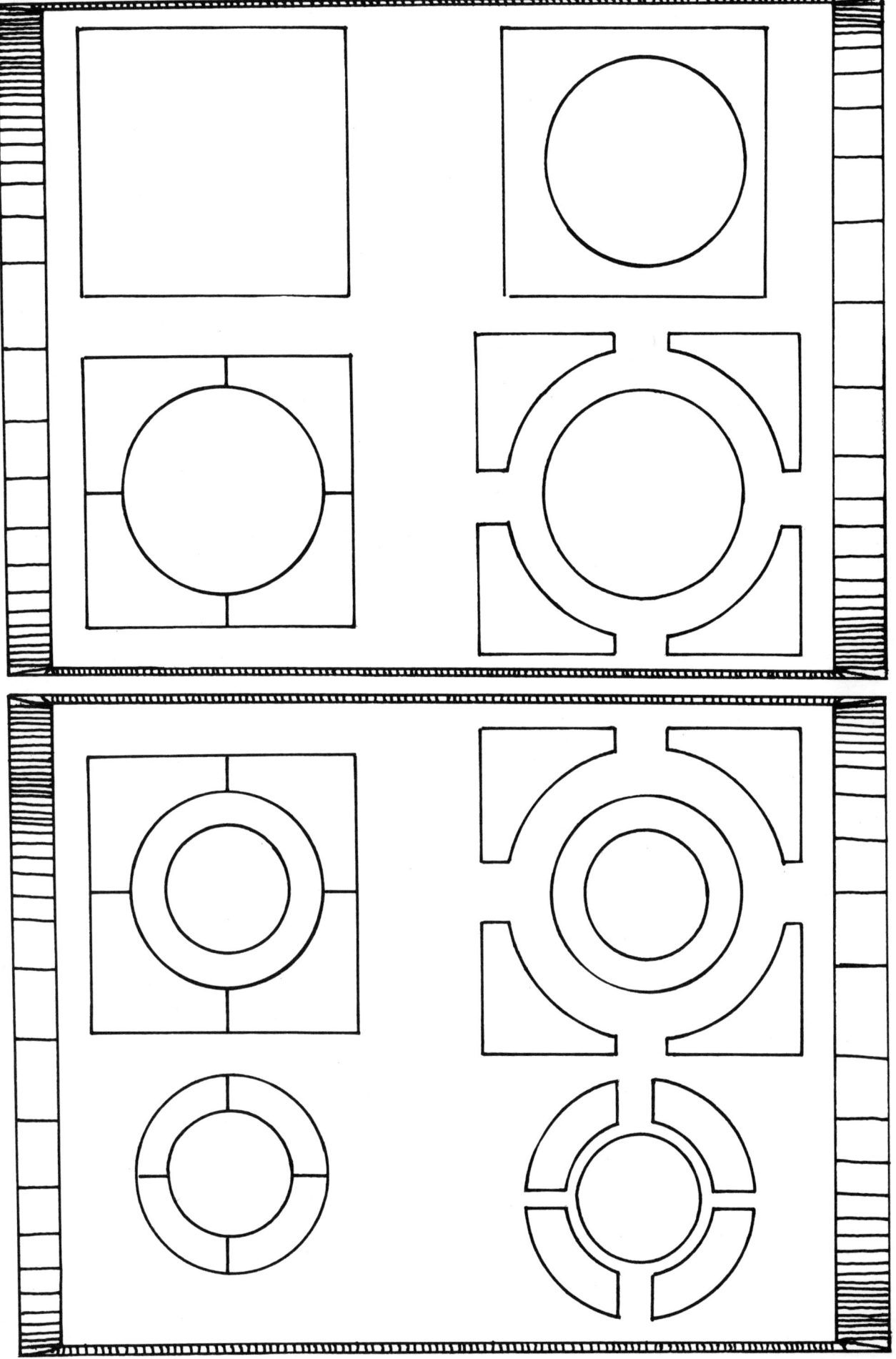

There are four steps to follow when using a lens cutter to cut a circle (Ill. 8-1):

(1) Measure the diameter of the circle and adjust the lens cutter. Then cut out a square piece of glass that measures slightly larger than the diameter of the desired circle.
(2) Place the glass square into position on the lens cutter; press down and turn the handle to score a circle.
(3) To separate the circle from the square, make four score lines that run from the circle's edge to the edges of the square (all opposite each other—either vertically/horizontally or diagonally).
(4) Break off the surrounding square.

To cut an arc with the lens cutter (Ill. 8-1):
(1) Cut out a glass square, and score a large circle and then a smaller circle within the large circle.
(2) Make four score lines that run from the larger circle's edge to the edges of the square and break off the square.
(3) Score the larger circle in four places.
(4) Break off the surrounding arcs.

All resulting shapes—circles, arcs, and surrounding squares—can be used in a design as they are or cut into various-size wedges. In case you think that your design choices are few when working with glass, consider the four window designs in Ill. 8-2; each piece in these windows can be cut with a lens cutter and a straightedge.

Templates

The *template* is a cutout pattern used as a guide for cutting nontransparent glass, repeat designs, and difficult curving shapes. Templates provide an accurate way of cutting glass and also save time and glass in return for the added trouble of making them. A template works best and lasts longest when cut from brass (with a jeweler's saw), but other materials can be used—stiff paper, cardboard, tin. As a general rule, the harder the material used, the better the template.

Compare having to separately measure, cut, and groze forty pieces of glass to cutting around a template forty times; or imagine having to guess at the exact shape of a piece and using up a full sheet of opaque glass in the trying. Templates are a professional solution for such situations.

You will often see stacks of glass arranged on the workbench at a glassworker's studio in piles of the same color and shape; they can be quickly assembled into a specific design. This glass will have been cut with the aid of templates that are normally kept taped together and filed away (with a copy of their design) when not in use. Templates were used to cut all of the lamps shown in the opening color photographs, with the exception of Gilly's work. Professionals don't have time or glass to squander—neither should you.

Once you have cut out a template, it can be used in different ways. One method is to lay the template over a rectangular piece of glass (slightly larger than the template) and cut around the pattern. Care must be taken not to shift the template or the glass while you are cutting, or the finished piece will be inaccurate. An alternative to this method is to lay the template over the rectangular piece of glass and outline the shape in pencil directly on the glass.

Ill. 8-2

Four rough sketches of windows—all of which can be cut with a lens or circle cutter, plus a straightedge or try square and an ordinary glass cutter.

The piece can then be cut freehand by following the lines on the glass. Stabilo glass pencils, made by Swan in Germany, are excellent for this purpose and will not smudge or interfere with cutting. White, yellow, and blue pencils will cover most of the range of colored glasses. However, a standard black pencil will do quite well in most cases.

One additional point to keep in mind when making templates is the degree of their accuracy. You should cut individual templates at least 1/16 inch smaller than the original design to compensate for the width of your cutter's wheel.

Ill. 8-3

One of the many designs most accurately cut with the aid of templates. This design, imitative of Valasco's work, employs pieces of the same width but of different lengths. By first cutting the glass into long strips of equal width, individual pieces can then be cut with their corresponding templates.

Chapter 9:

LAMP CONSTRUCTION

Before getting into the step-by-step details of lamp construction, it is good to have a general overview of what is involved in making a lamp. The problem is to construct a six-paneled (six-sided), hanging lamp. The procedure is much the same for all hanging (or standing) lamps of this type—whether they are made of six, twelve, twenty-four, or even thirty-six panels. Before reading further, flip through the next six pages of illustrations to understand how a lamp grows.

Preliminary Work

The first panel (Ill. 9-1) has been drawn to size to expedite construction. Make a tracing of this panel and use it to make a template (from brass, tin, cardboard, etc.). Once you have the template, use it to make a drawing of the lamp laid out (Ill. 9-2). This drawing is needed for placing newly cut pieces of glass in their correct positions. Decide upon a design, copy it onto the drawing, and cut up the template accordingly. Finally, cut, wrap, and reassemble all the glass for the lamp shade.

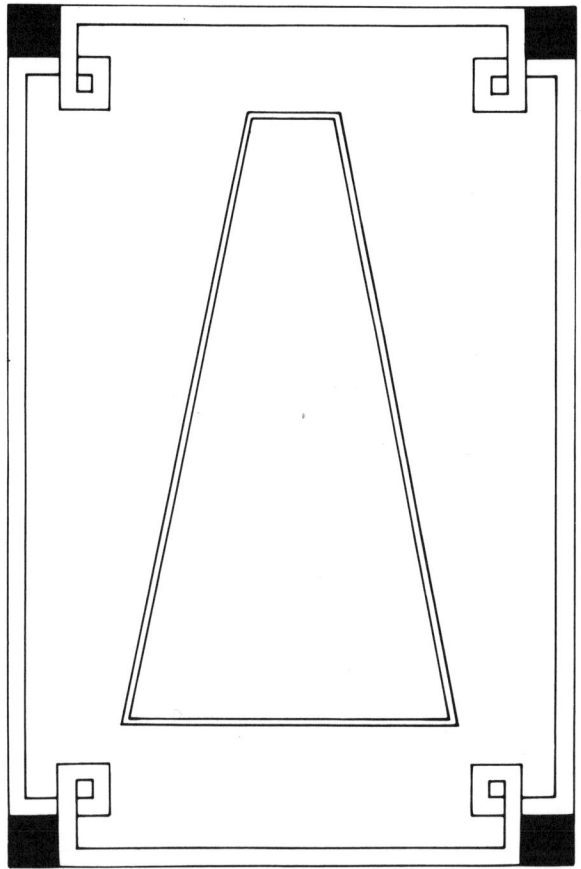

Ill. 9-1

The first panel of a lamp drawn to correct dimensions.

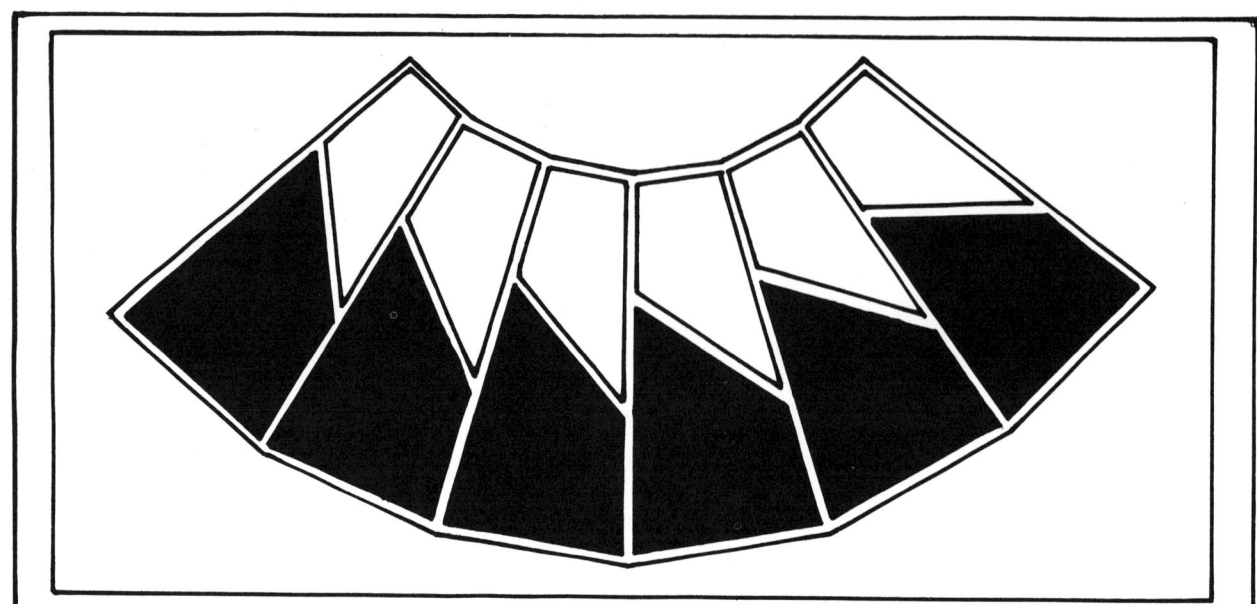

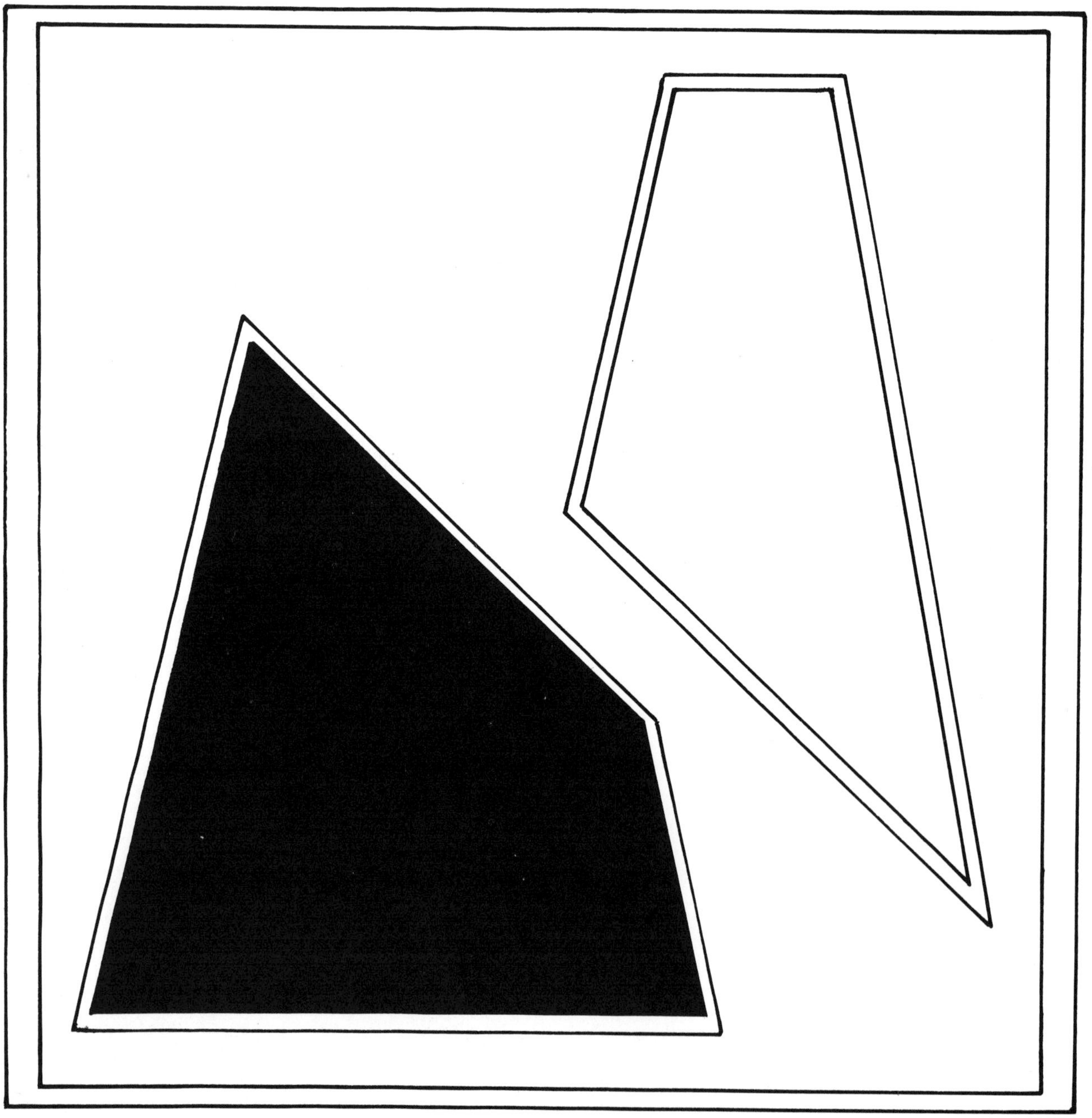

Ill. 9-2

A lamp drawn and laid out in two dimensions with its interior design shaded in *(top),* and the two templates—drawn full-scale—used for cutting the panels *(bottom).*

Soldering

When you are ready to solder, treat each panel separately so that only the internal design has a finished bead on both faces. *Do not solder the perimeters, because this will interfere with joining the panels.*

Arrange the panels over a piece of paper with the base edges touching each other (Ill. 9-3) and then outline the resulting shape. Remove this drawing and surround it with a wall of support nails. Take two panels, place them against the support nails, and lift them into position (Ill. 9-4). This step ensures that your panels meet at the proper angles. Tack the panels together, add another panel, tack it, add, tack, etc., until all six panels have been tacked into position.

Next tin the exterior and interior joints. (Don't worry if the newly added solder runs or streaks over previously soldered lines. It will not stick if you have wiped off the excess flux beforehand.) After you have tinned the joints together, you are ready to lay the finished bead. To do this, you will need wooden supports to hold the joint to be soldered parallel to the work surface (Ill. 9-5). Bead the interior joints first; do one, turn the lamp, do another one, turn, another, etc. After finishing the interior, rest the shade against the lath strip on your work surface and prop it up with blocks of wood. Again, do one joint, turn the shade, do another, etc. The final perimeter soldering is accomplished quite easily—without a need for supports. Wipe the entire lamp to remove excess solder, turn the shade upright, and solder the top perimeter. Then turn the shade upside down and solder the base perimeter.

Ill. 9-3 *(page 76)*

The six panels of a lamp arranged to locate the base perimeter *(top),* and a drawing of the base perimeter surrounded with support nails *(bottom).*

Ill. 9-4 *(page 77)*

The first two panels as they are tacked together over a drawing of the base perimeter. Note that the nails are on the outside of the glass.

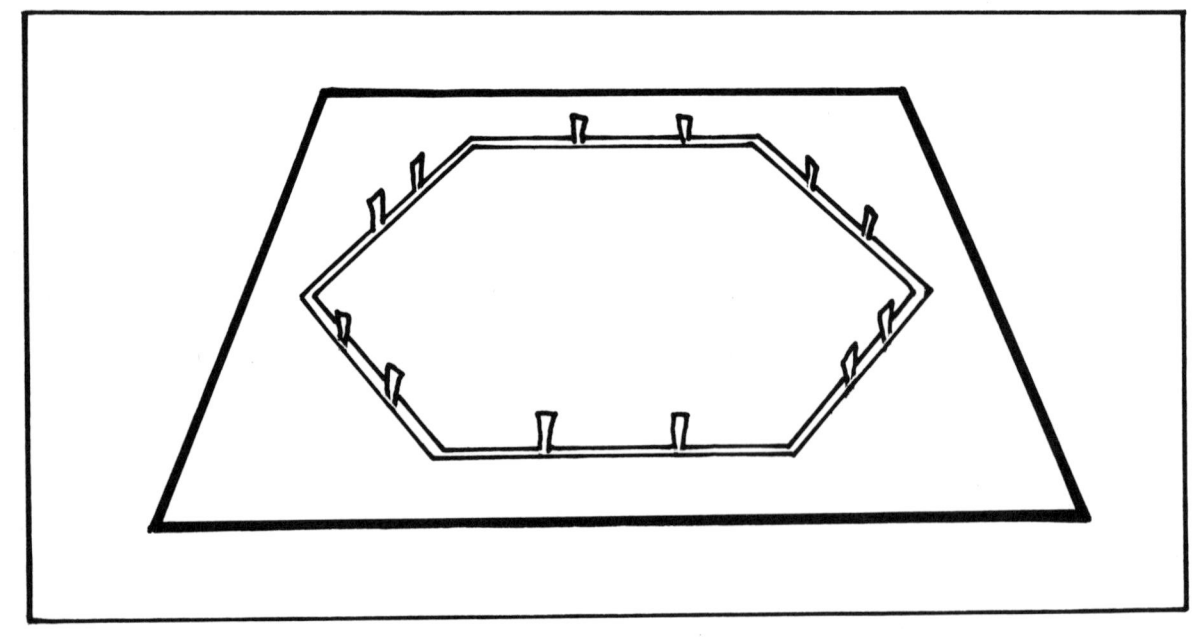

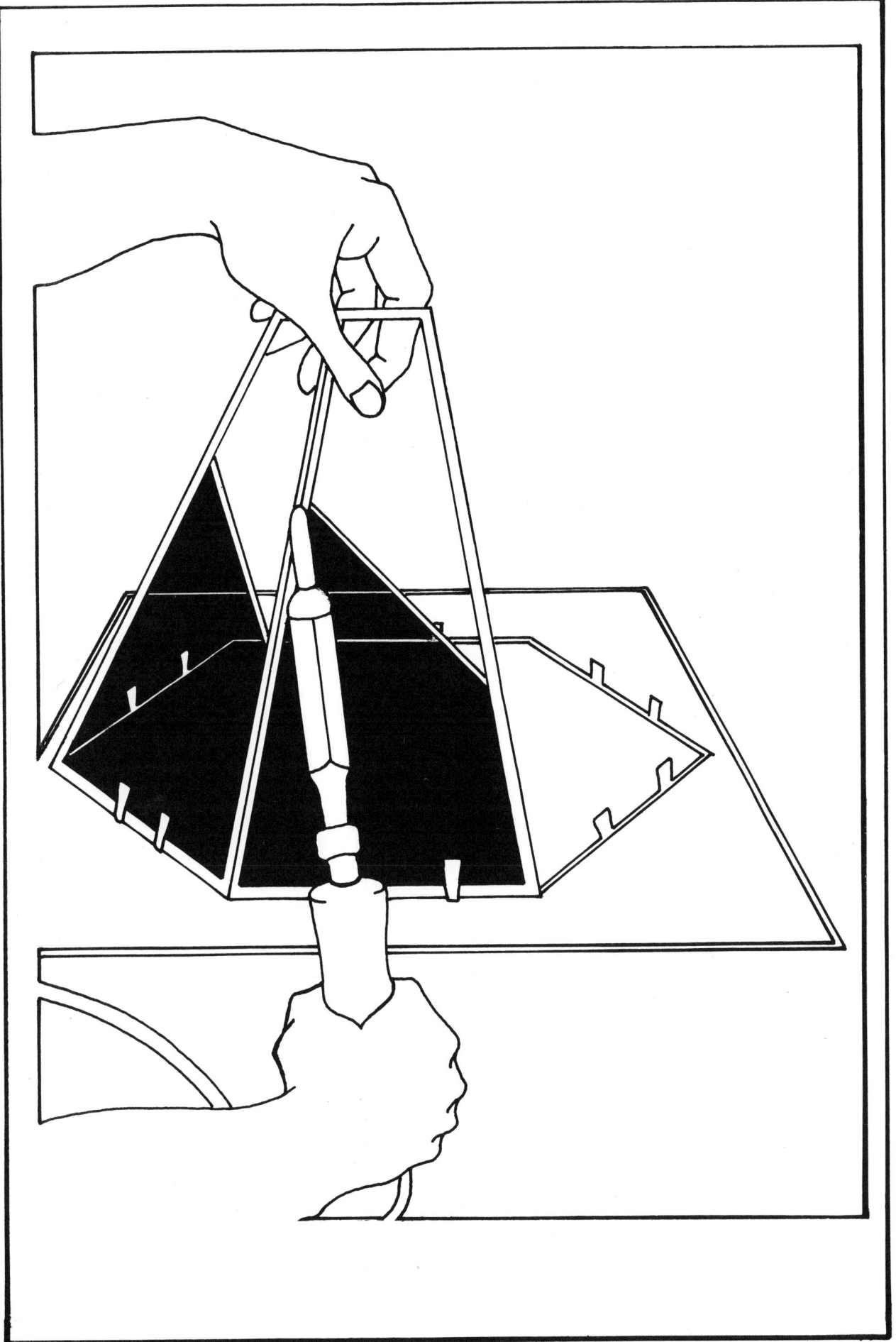

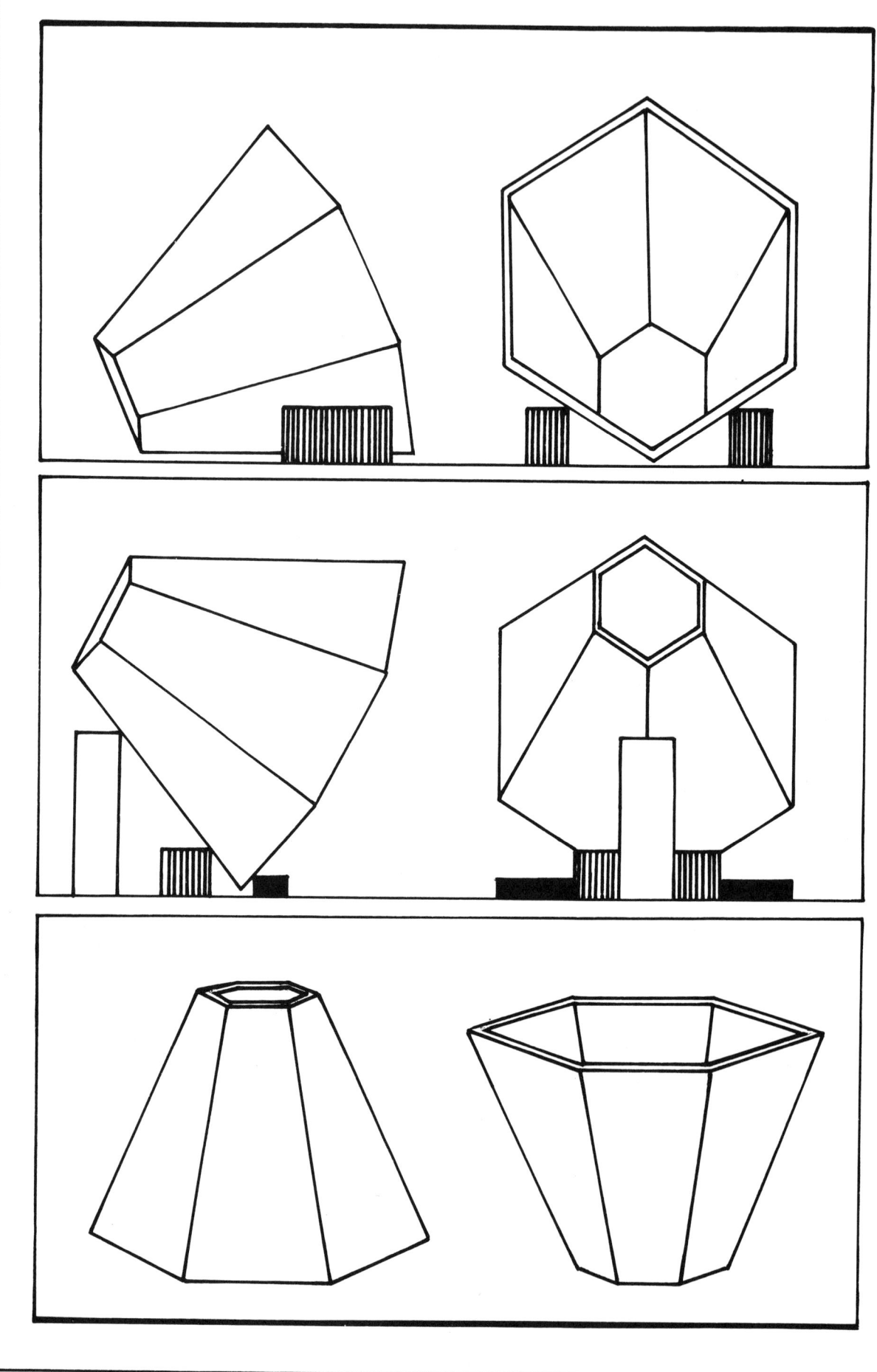

Ill. 9-5

At top, a side and a bottom view of a lamp shade, resting on two blocks of wood and ready for interior soldering. At center, a side and a top view of the shade ready for exterior soldering; its bottom perimeter presses against the work surface's lath strip, while two blocks of wood support it (the tallest block should have a V-shaped notch cut into it). At bottom, the positions for soldering the top and base perimeters.

Assembly

You can purchase all the lamp components through your glass supplier or at a lighting-supply store. You will need the following items:

chain pliers
wire cutters
brass chain
brass hanging loop
brass hanging hook
brass nipple (approximately one inch long)
brass or porcelain socket (either use a pull chain or attach an on/off switch to the zip cord)
two brass vase caps (one slightly larger than the other)
two brass hexagonal locknuts and locking washers
brass-colored zip cord
plug

The metal components are all screwed onto the nipple in this order (Ill. 9-6):

hanging loop
locknut
locking washer
(smaller)* vase cap
lamp shade
(larger)* vase cap
locknut
locking washer
socket

*For some lamps, these caps may be reversed. In other words, the larger first, then the smaller. The correct order depends on the angles at the top of individual shades.

Attach one end of the chain to the hanging loop. Weave the zip cord through the chain, then pass it through the metal components, and attach it to the socket. Tighten everything together and take up any slack in the zip cord at the plug end. Hang the chain from a hanging hook placed in the ceiling and remove any excess chain. Run the zip cord to the nearest outlet, cut off any excess cord, and attach a plug. Always allow enough cord to reach the outlet after the plug is attached.

As an alternative to sandwiching the shade between two vase caps, it is simpler on small (six-paneled) lamps to solder just one vase cap onto the shade. However you decide to assemble your lamp, take your first shade with you when you buy your components—because they all come in graduated sizes.

Ill. 9-6 *(page 80)*

The shade and lamp components before and after tightening.

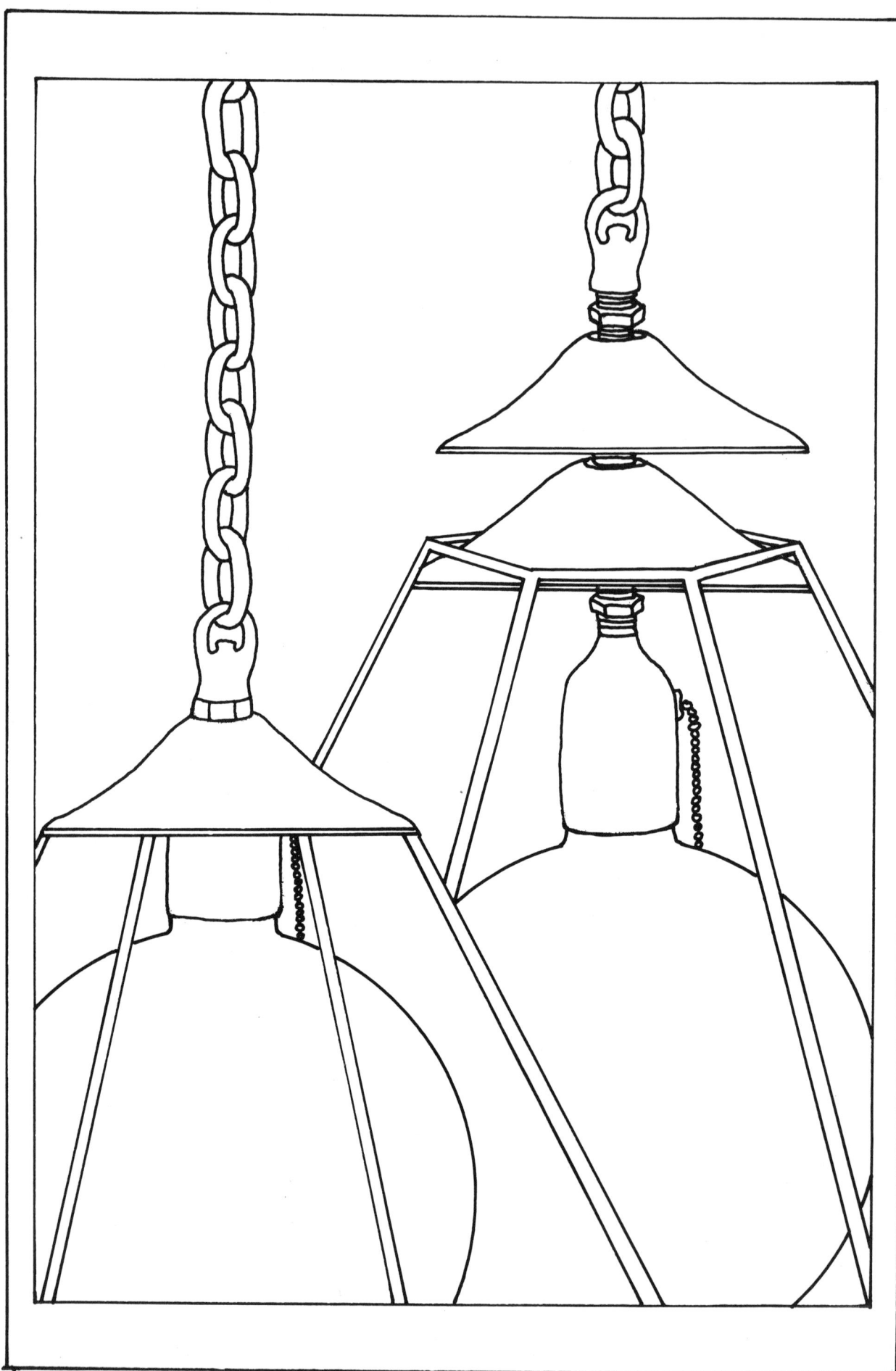

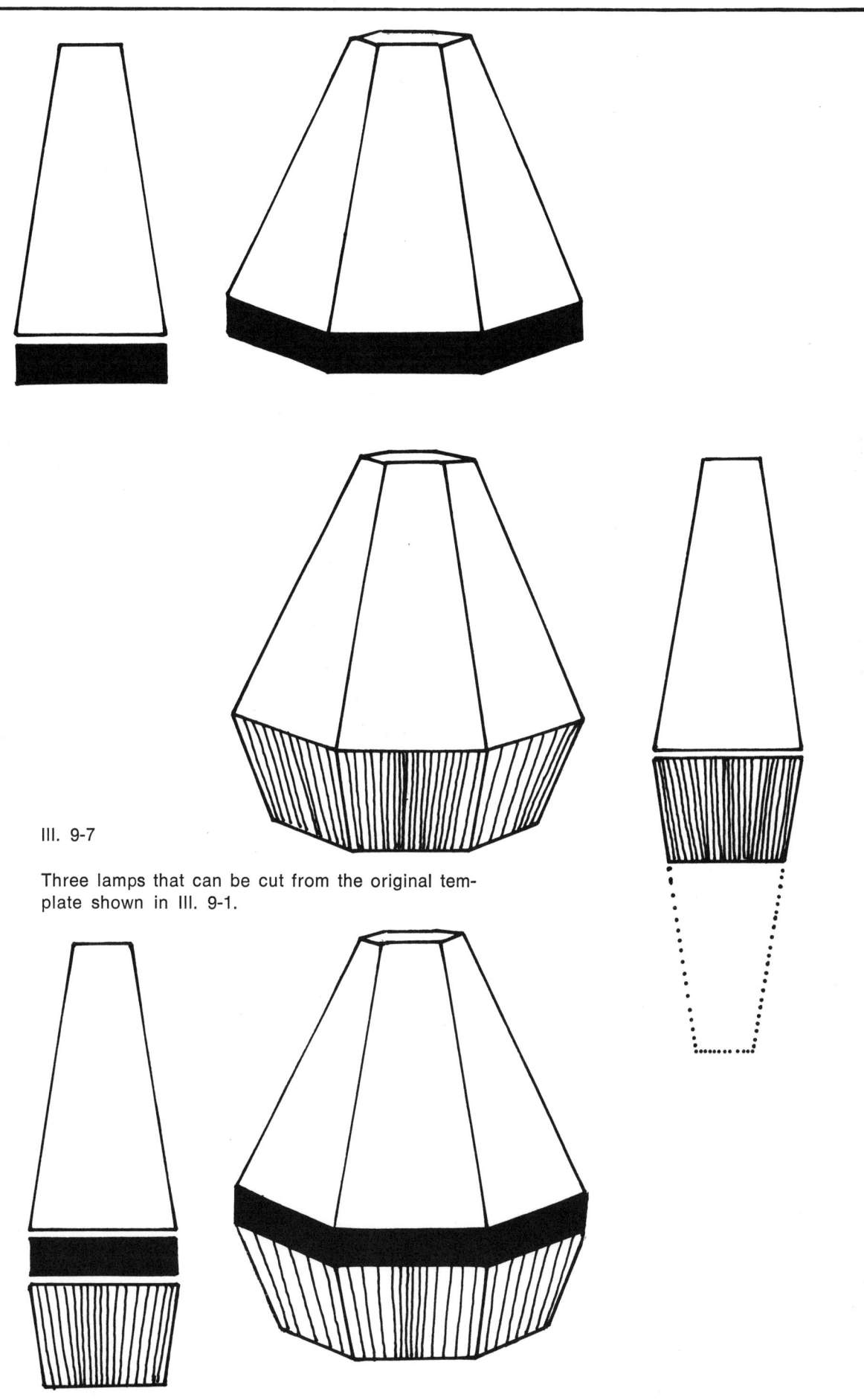

Ill. 9-7

Three lamps that can be cut from the original template shown in Ill. 9-1.

Light Bulbs

Ideally, a lamp is both a functional item and a beautiful object. A problem arises, however, in the lighting. The aim should be to light the maximum area of glass without blinding the observer or creating hot spots (areas of concentrated light) on the lamp surface. One way to eliminate glare if the lamp is hung above eye level is to use a bulb that is silver-coated on the bottom.

Using a single, coated light bulb in a stained-glass lamp is, at best, a speedy solution. If you must use a single bulb, then experiment with the uncoated variety. These bulbs, even at forty watts, throw an especially brilliant light and can be purchased in many different shapes—huge globe, elongated tube, short, fat, even squarish. Also, depending upon the shape of the lamp, you might want to use more than one bulb; instead of using a single seventy-five-watt bulb, try using three twenty-five-watt bulbs.

Glass Densities

As mentioned earlier in Chapter 2, glass is purchased not only for its color but also for its texture and density. When choosing glass for a lamp, keep the glare of the bulb in mind and select the best possible combinations of glass between transparent and opaque—one for the freedom of light and the other as a shield against it. As usual, the quickest solution—to use exclusively opalescent glass—is the least interesting. Even completely transparent glass can be used at eye level as long as it is surrounded by translucent and semiopaque glasses. Once above eye level or below bulb level, transparent glass can be used at liberty. Look for the exact point at which the type of bulb, number of bulbs, glass density, and hanging (or standing) level coincide perfectly. More often than not, you will find it.

One final note: anything that can be wrapped in copperfoil and soldered without damage can be used as a part or the whole of a lamp or panel. For example, instead of using a circle cut from sheet glass, use a rondel or bullseye (round pieces of glass having thick, raised centers). Or replace a square, diamond, circle, or oval shape with a faceted glass jewel (thick pieces of glass cut to imitate jewels) of corresponding size and shape. In fact, if you look closely at Gilly's work in the opening color photographs, you will notice that he has used all of the above, plus mirrors, prisms, car headlights, reflectors, and even whole bottles, glass nuggets, and industrial glass. Apart from the glass objects that can be used, sliced cuts of semiprecious stones or sections of iridescent shells can act as an excellent substitute for opal glass.

By working with a variety of materials, you approach a form of sculpting—the piece evolves as you work rather than conforming to a preconceived idea. This approach also encourages the use of open spaces within a design. Instead of a purely superficial examination of a flat surface, you can be a good light magician and lead the eye into and over the entire design.

III. 9-8

Two twelve-paneled lamps and three six-paneled lamps—all made from the sample pattern in III. 9-1. Except for the lamp that is hanging, all the panels of these lamps are exactly the same size. The panels of the hanging lamp are about one inch longer at top and bottom than the original pattern, and this lamp also sports a double skirt.

Chapter 10:

DESIGNING ORIGINAL LAMPS

Eventually this chapter may be the most interesting and challenging part of this book, but chances are that you will not need its information immediately. It will probably become valuable after you have made a few panels and a couple of simple lamps.

Before I learned how to figure out my lamp dimensions, I used a pattern that a friend had given to me, and I just copied it over and over again until I eventually bored myself silly. By the time I reached that point, I had taken the original pattern and lengthened it, widened it, increased its panels from six to twelve, and added skirts—even double skirts. This whole process was not unlike the program I presented in the previous chapter.

When I reached the limits of the original design—when adaptations no longer challenged me—I wanted much more freedom in designing. I wanted to have radical control over basic design and not just creative manipulation of the same simple shape.

Now I usually begin a new lamp by saying to myself, "I want a lamp that is about ten inches high, fifteen inches wide at its broadest point, four inches wide at its top opening, and about eight inches wide at its bottom." Once I have made these decisions—based on a particular room or setting—I can go ahead and design the lamp on graph paper, make my templates, and finally cut the lamp's glass pieces. And all of the measurements in these three steps will be accurate to one-sixteenth of an inch.

The designing process is easy enough, requiring only a ruler, graph paper, a protractor, and the ability to count. It is not even time-consuming—in fact, it takes longer to explain the process than to do it. You can design a lamp on paper in fifteen minutes, as opposed to the hours you could spend making a paper model, correcting it, making another model, etc.

Briefly, here is the process. First take a rough sketch and transfer it onto graph paper. From this proportional drawing on the graph paper you make actual-size drawings of the lamp. By measuring lines on the actual-size drawings and combining them, you can obtain the individual panel measurements that are used to make templates. These, in turn, are used to cut the glass. By using graph paper for all drawings from sketch to templates, you don't have to check whether your lines are parallel and perpendicular to each other.

The following detailed explanation is in two parts. The first consists of four diagrams and a corresponding text that tells you how to make the necessary semitechnical drawings for a lamp. The second part explains how to use such drawings to construct a lamp. If you are familiar with graph-paper work or have a penchant for it, you can quickly skim over the first part and move on to the second. Because lamp designing is a visual process, both parts demand a close reading of the text with continual references to the illustrations.

In order to illustrate this design process, throughout this chapter I have used one sample lamp, which is pictured in Ill. 10-1 (side view) and Ill. 10-2 (top view). My purpose in using this lamp is to show you how to design your own lamps—not just to give you another model to copy.

Ill. 10-1 *(above)*

Side view of the actual sample lamp—complete except for wiring.

Ill. 10-2 *(below)*

Top view of the completed sample lamp.

Part One:

Working Drawings

You need three working drawings from side and top for each paneled lamp that you design. If Ill. 10-3, which shows these three drawings, is at all confusing, go on to Ills. 10-4, 10-5, and 10-6. Use Ill. 10-3 as a reference point. Ill. 10-4 is a side view of the sample lamp that will be used throughout this explanation. To understand the perspective of the drawing, imagine slicing through the lamp sideways.

When you transfer a rough sketch to graph paper, your first line is the center vertical or height of the lamp. The next group of lines includes the horizontals or widths of the lamp. By connecting their ends, you form the basic lamp shape.

To work out an interior design within these extremities, draw in four or six panels. This is done by locating center points along each horizontal line and then connecting these points. After you have drawn an interior design, you might want to shade in different areas to get a better sense of the finished lamp.

Ill. 10-3

The three working drawings, all drawn to scale: at top, a full side view of the lamp; at left, a half side view; and at right, half of the top view.

Ill. 10-4

A step-by-step drawing of the side view, as if taken from a rough sketch and transferred to graph paper.

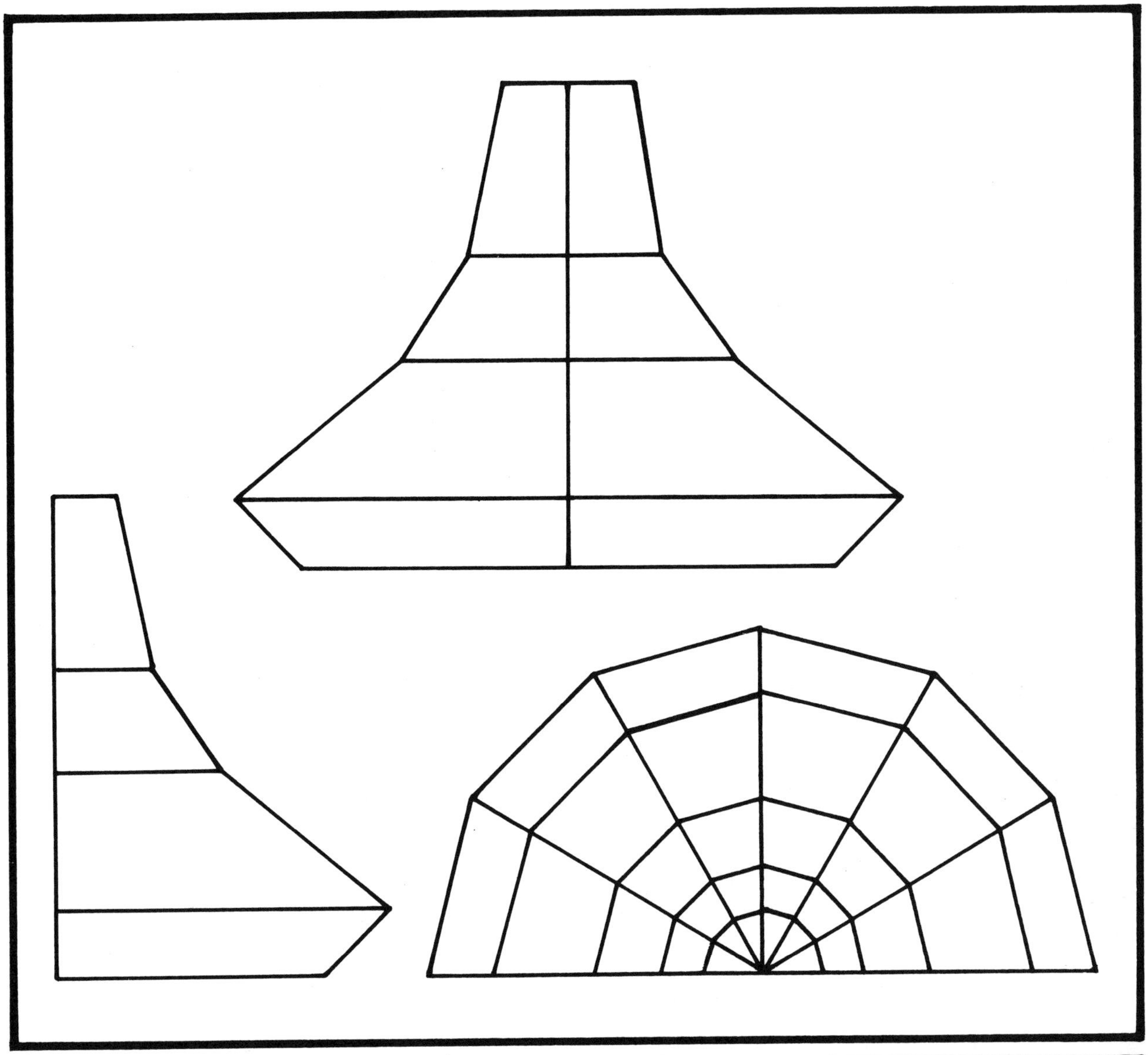

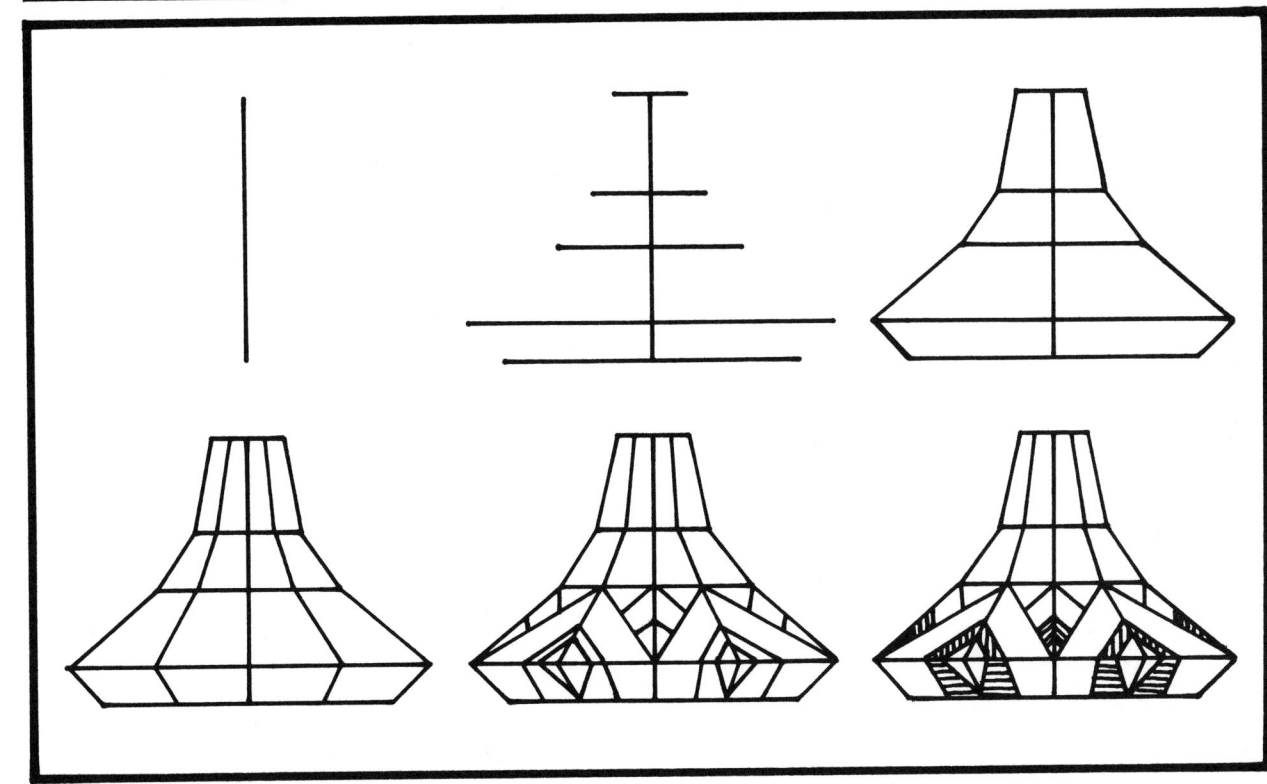

Ill. 10-5 is a top view of the same lamp. If you were to stand above this lamp and look down on it, it would look very much like the drawing—except not quite so perfectly defined, since the lamp would be in three dimensions and the drawing is in two. To clarify what this drawing represents, look at Ill. 10-6. It shows how the two views (side and top) are related to each other—on both the design (right side) and the working-drawing (left side) levels. Another way of understanding this is to look at something else in the two different positions—a cup or glass will do. Remember that you are looking down on something, which is shortened or distorted in this perspective.

Now return is Ill. 10-5. In a top view, a twelve-sided lamp forms a near circle, which geometrically is called a polygon. Since there are 360 degrees in a circle, if you divide twelve (the twelve sides) into 360 degress, you get 30 degrees. In the same way, if you wanted an eighteen-sided lamp, you would divide eighteen into 360 degrees and get 20 degrees. What this means for our purposes is that the twelve sides of the lamp are coming together at an angle of 30 degrees to each other. The first line you draw for this illustration is as long as the lamp is wide at its broadest point. (Check Ill. 10-6 if you are not sure.) As the drawing progresses, five more lines of that exact length will cross each other at their center points, giving you a total of six lines crossing each other. Or, instead of six lines crossing each other, twelve short lines meet at a central point. Whichever way you choose to see it, all the lines are 30 degrees apart from each other. The lines that transform the star shape into the polygon shape designate the individual panel widths—remember the foreshortening factor in a top view.

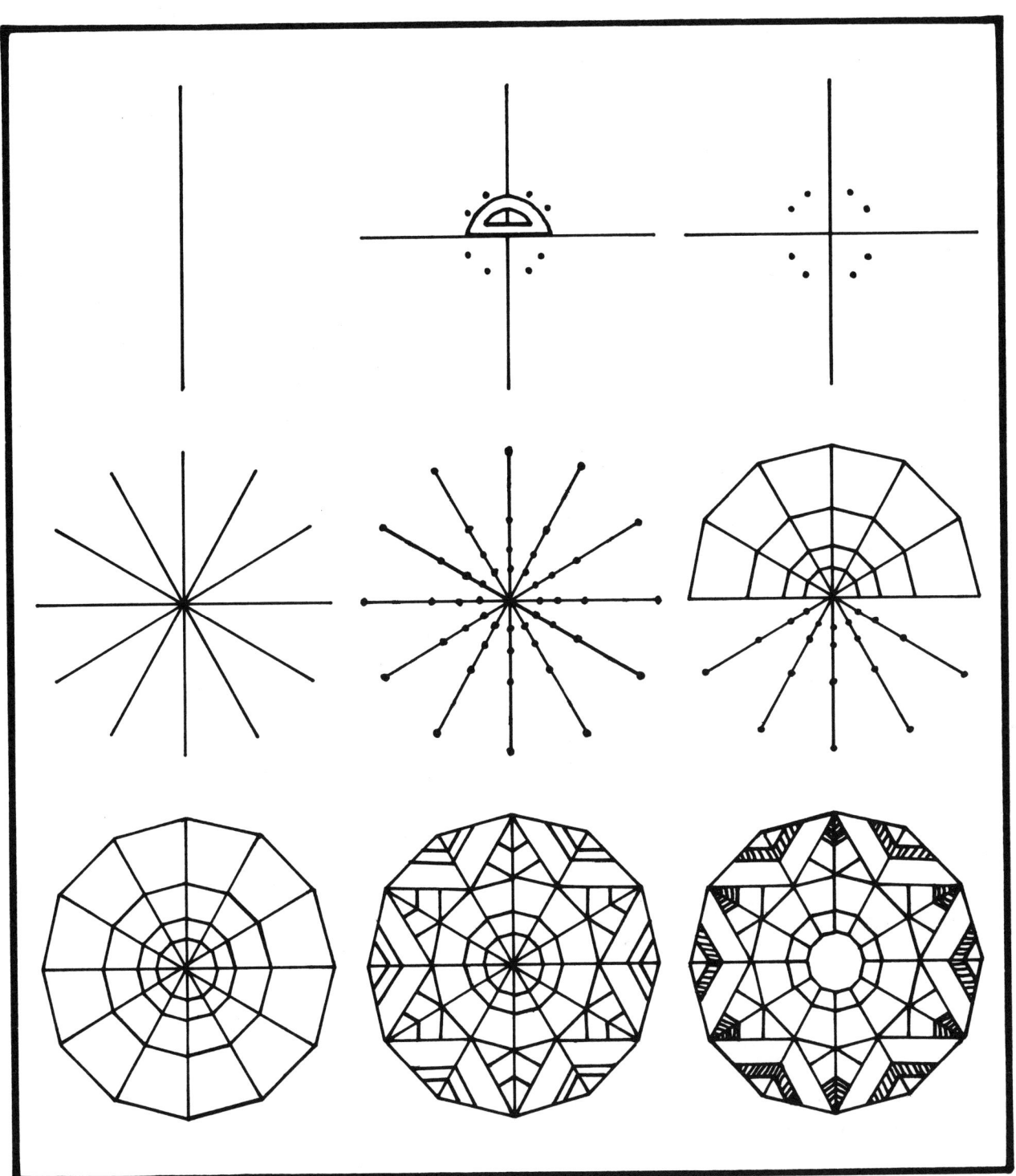

Ill. 10-5

A step-by-step drawing of the top view, constructed with the aid of a ruler and protractor.

Besides illustrating the relationship between the top and side views, Ill. 10-6 points up another interesting and important change. Compare the two sides of this drawing. Notice that on the shaded side you cannot see the bottommost section of the lamp; it becomes invisible when the lamp is viewed from the top. Also notice that on the left, the working side of the diagram, the bottommost section of the lamp is now represented with a drawn line—as if the glass were totally transparent. In a finished lamp, that line does occur where it is drawn, except that it is a few inches lower. Do not let the arrows in this illustration confuse you; if you follow them to the bottom diagram you will see that they refer to the length of the line from the center to the edge of the lamp. The longest measurement is ten inches from center to outermost point (see top drawing). The next measurement along the same line occurs at eight inches from the center, the next is five inches from the center, etc. In this way, each of the twelve ten-inch-long lines will have marks at eight, five, three, and two inches respectively. By connecting these marks, you form the polygon shape of the lamp as it is seen from the top view.

Ill. 10-6

The side and top views and their relationship to each other: the left-hand side is the working-drawing level, while the right-hand side shows design shadings.

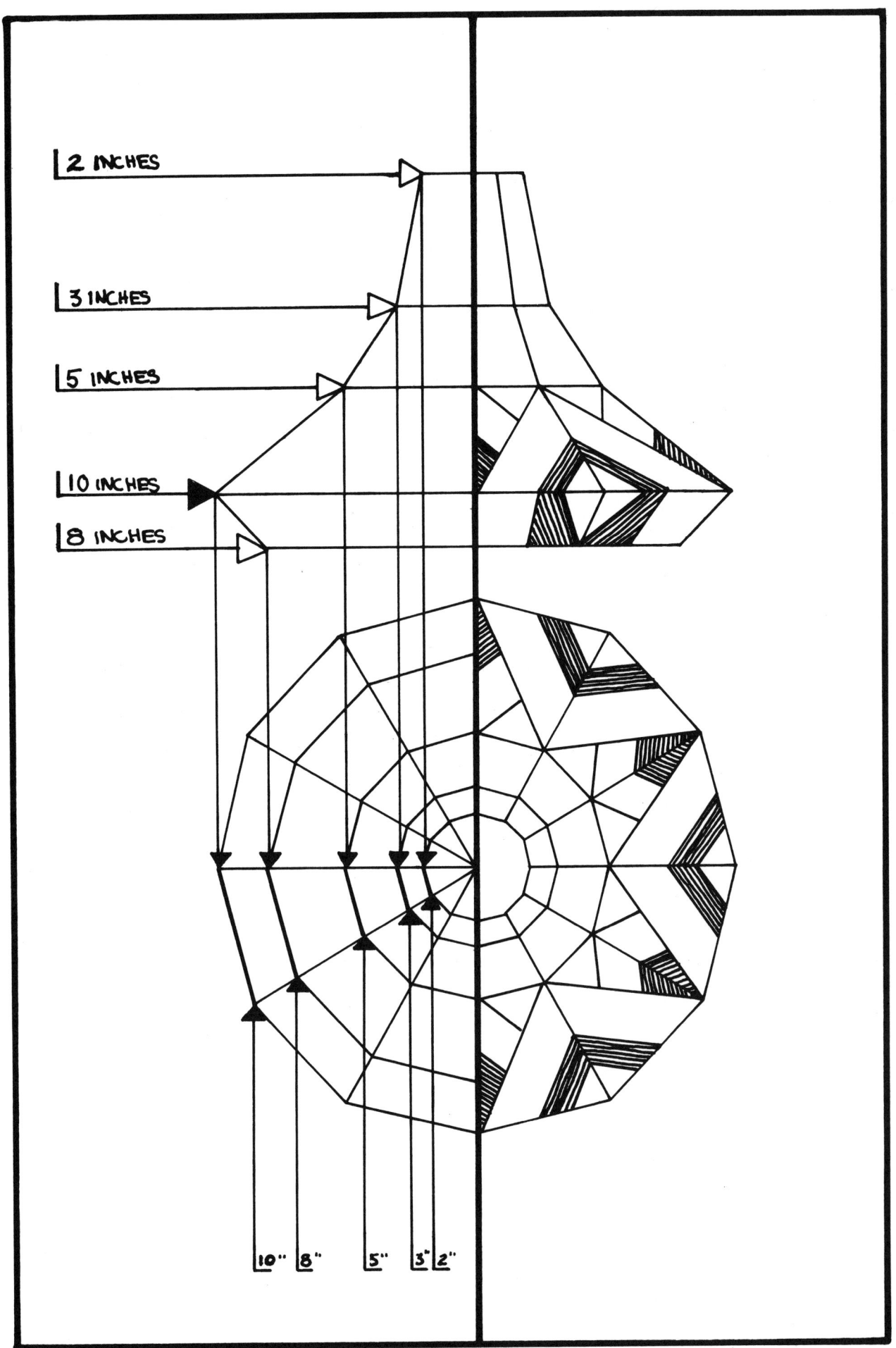

Part Two:

Construction Drawings

Once the process of graph-paper designing is understood, you can move on to the actual application of such designs to lamp construction. Ill. 10-7 returns to the beginning—a graph-paper sketch and the important measurements. Notice that the illustration is identical to the full side view of the design in Ill. 10-3. Since it is a line-for-line duplicate of a lamp that I designed and cut in glass, you can check my figures by counting the vertical and horizontal boxes in the illustration. Here, each box represents one inch, but you might decide to use two boxes to equal one inch, or three boxes, or even four, depending on the scale you want.

Ill. 10-8 returns to the first (full side) and second (half side) working drawings and shows how they are related to each other. The important cutting measurements are taken from the slopes of the sides of the lamp, where I have placed dashes. You might assume that measuring to one-sixteenth of an inch is a complicated way of measuring—it is not. It simplifies later work so much that I express all measurements in sixteenths. Ill. 10-9 relates the first (full side) and third (half top) working drawings. Again, the dashes show where to take the important measurements. Finally, Ills. 10-10 to 10-13 are actual-size drawings. They show how the individual panels are formed and how each section will look when tinned together.

When making these actual-size construction drawings, all of the height measurements are taken from Ill. 10-8, and all of the widths are taken from Ill. 10-9. Draw the height of the panel first, then the top and bottom widths, and finally connect their extremities to form the panel. Measuring to one-sixteenth of an inch comes in handy here. The height of each panel must be directly in the middle of the top and bottom widths, or the completed panel will be lopsided. This means that each width measurement on all of these construction drawings must be divided in half. For example, the width of the top of each panel of the lamp's first section measures 1 1/16 inches, or 8.5/16 inch on either side of the height measurement (Ill. 10-10). Likewise, the bottom width, 1 9/16 inches, becomes two sets of 12.5/16 inch, and on the next panel (Ill. 10-11) 2 9/16 inches becomes two sets of 1 4.5/16 inches, etc. It is even more accurate to work to the thirty-second of an inch rather than by my unambitious method—in which case the two sets of 1 4.5/16 inches become two sets of 1 9/32 inches. Some super-scrupulous designers even work to a sixty-fourth of an inch; fractional examples of these I leave to your own figuring.

Since graph paper ensures that all your lines will be perfectly straight and perpendicular to each other, you can glue these actual-size drawings onto pieces of hard cardboard to use as your templates for cutting glass. Once the glue has dried, cut around the shape with a ruler and a razor blade. Use the cardboard to trace the shape onto the glass with a Stabilo glass pencil or to make a metal template.

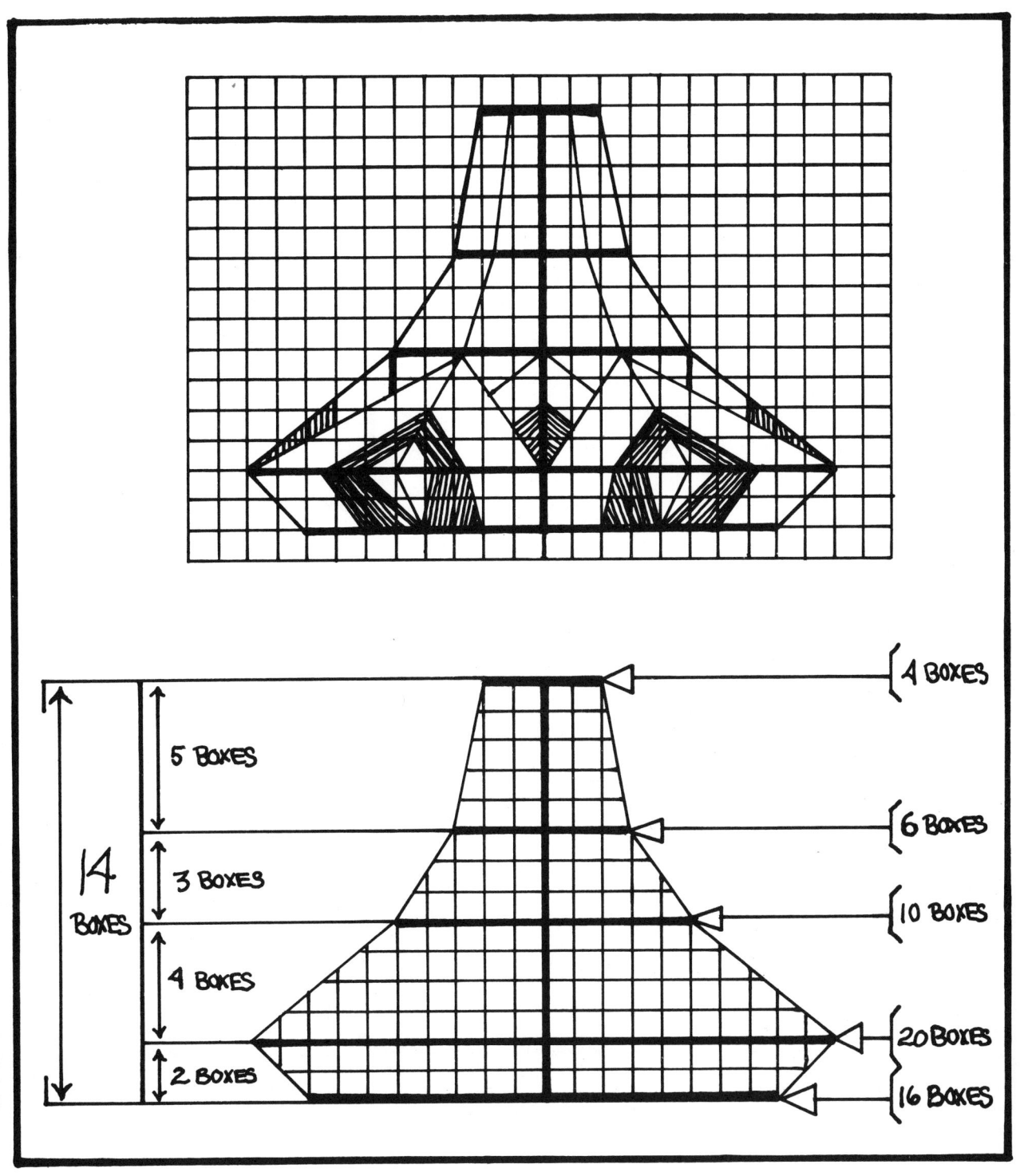

III. 10-7

The lamp worked out on graph paper with its measurements in boxes. The scale is one box to one inch.

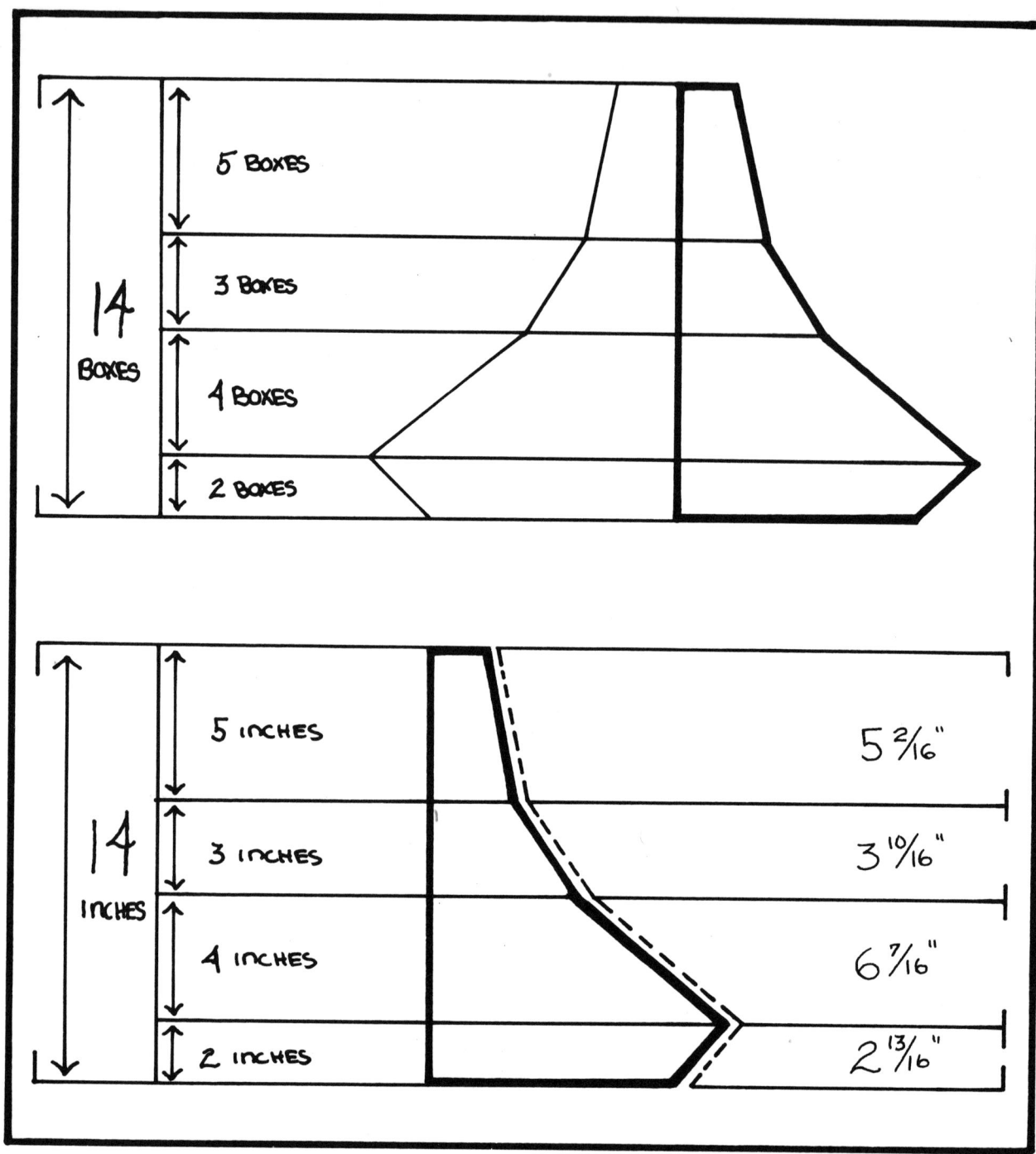

III. 10-8

Construction drawing from which the lamp's heights are obtained by measuring along lines indicated by dashes.

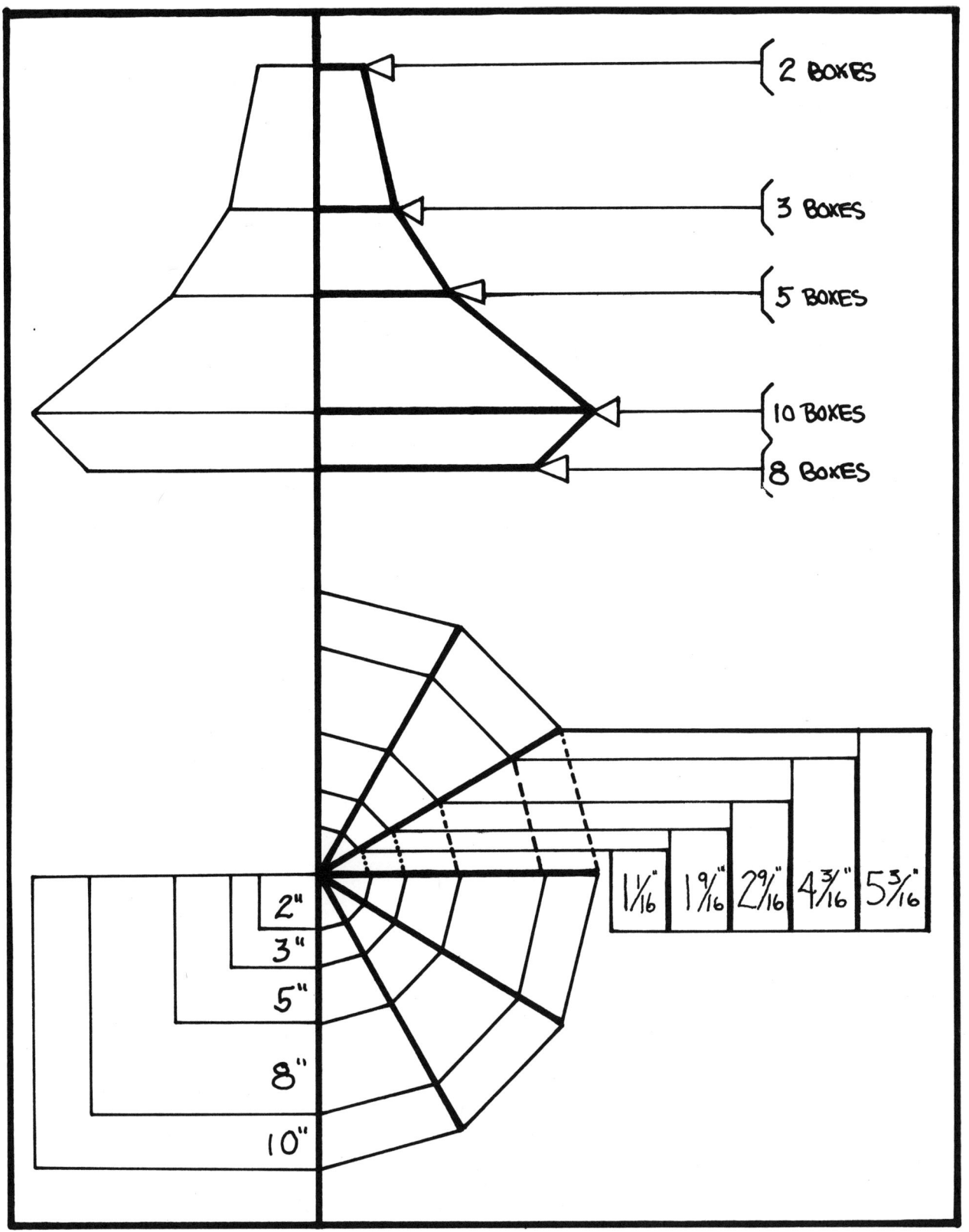

Ill. 10-9

Construction drawing from which the lamp's widths are taken.

Assembly

Even though you check, cross-check, and make corrections for cutting inaccuracies, you will never be machine-perfect. Every little error—let alone the big ones—will eventually show up when you start to assemble the lamp. On the other hand, every small correction will also be apparent—but only to you. No one else will know about that extra fifteen minutes spent on grozing that saved you all kinds of trouble and frustration, nor will they care—but you will. Every multilevel panel lamp will vary slightly when it comes to final assembly, but you will generally have to tackle the hardest part first and then make adjustments by manipulating the easier sections.

The sample lamp was assembled in the following way (see Ills. 10-10–10-13): I tinned together the panels of section 1 and set it aside, then I tinned the panels of section 2 together and also set it aside. When I reached section 3, I ran into my first problem. The individual panels of that section were quite heavy, because they each had an interior design that was soldered together with a finished bead. The combined weight of these panels and the angle at which they had to be soldered together tended to pull the tinned joints apart. As a result, this section was too fragile to be worked upon easily. To correct this weakness, I soldered section 2 to section 3. Once they were tinned together, I put a finished bead onto the interior and exterior joints of both sections. Next I attached section 4 to section 3 and added the finished bead. The last section attached to the lamp was section 1. Adjustments made along the way ensured that the design lines matched up for all four sections. It always takes a bit of playing by ear, but if your cutting work has been fairly accurate, the lamp will always fit together.

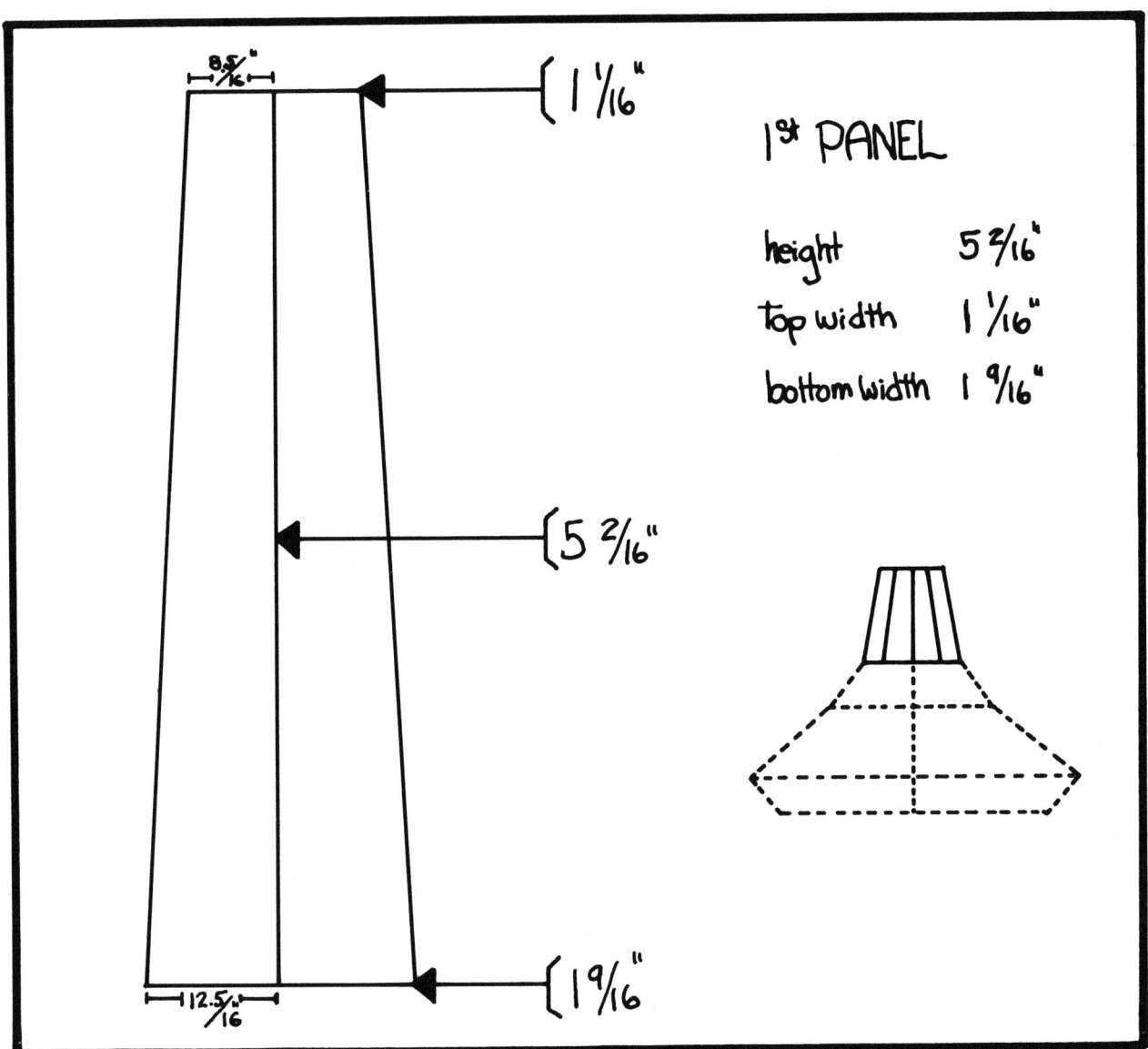

Ill. 10-10

The formation of the first panel in actual size from measurements taken from Ills. 10-8 and 10-9. The small model shows where the first panels—section 1—will appear on the soldered lamp.

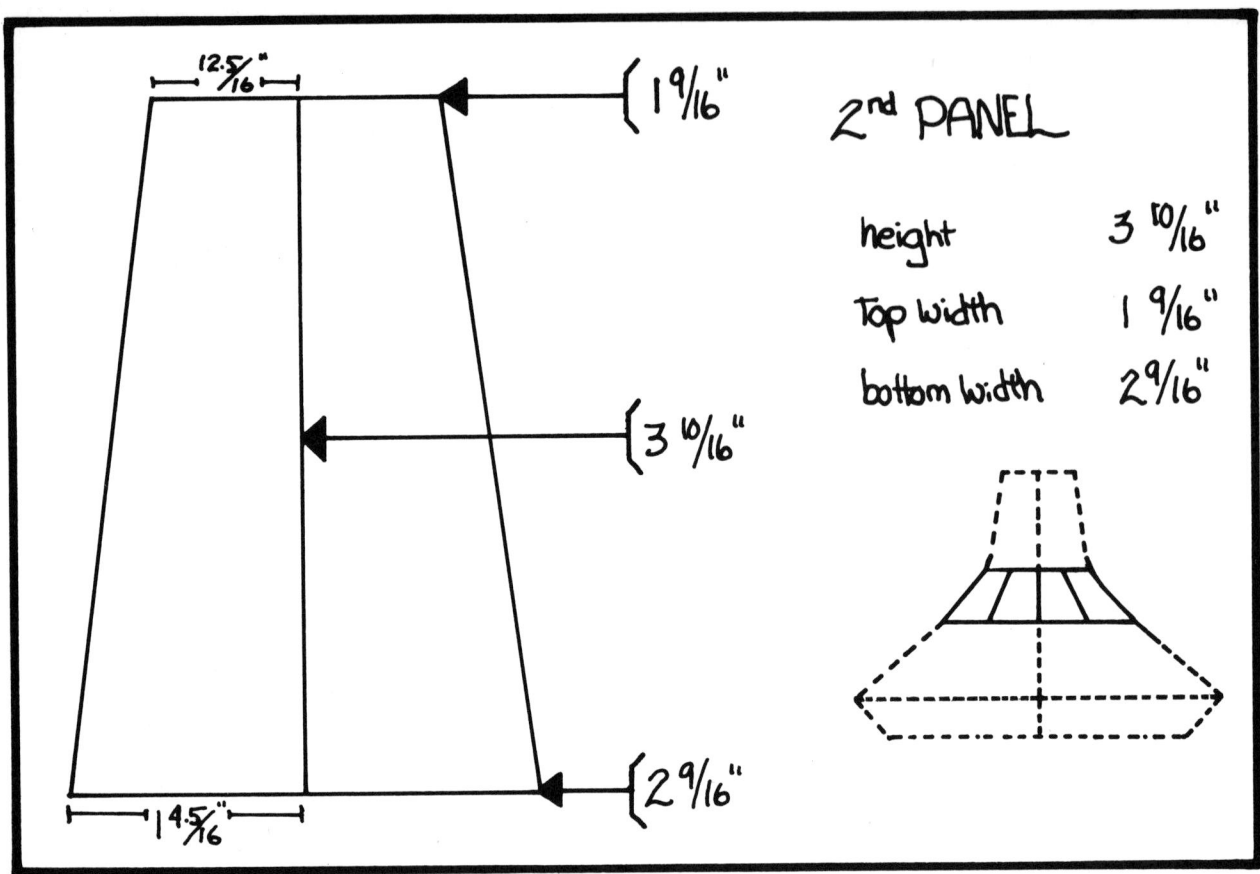

Ill. 10-11

Formation of the individual panels of section 2 of the lamp.

Ill. 10-12

The panels of section 3.

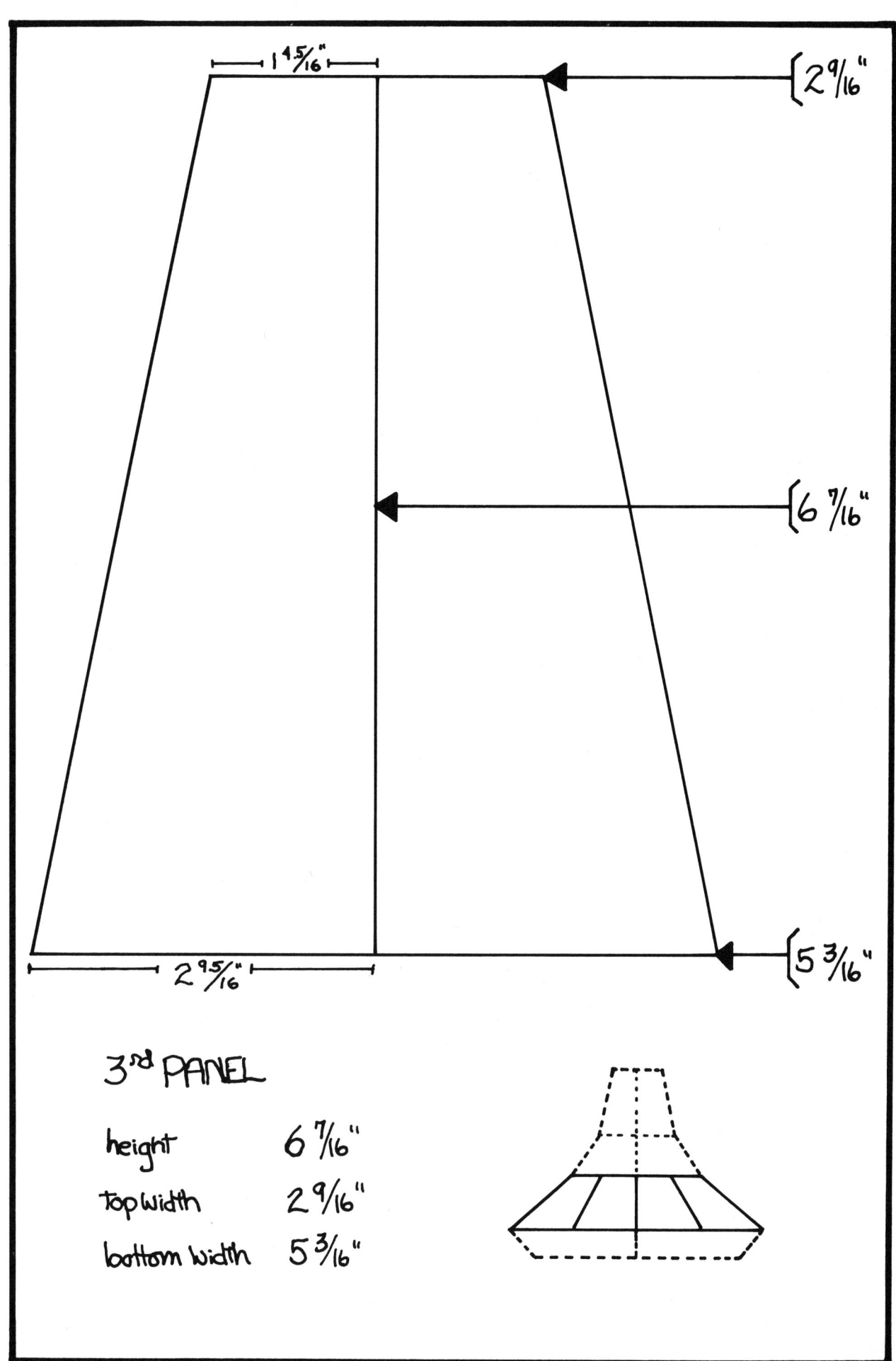

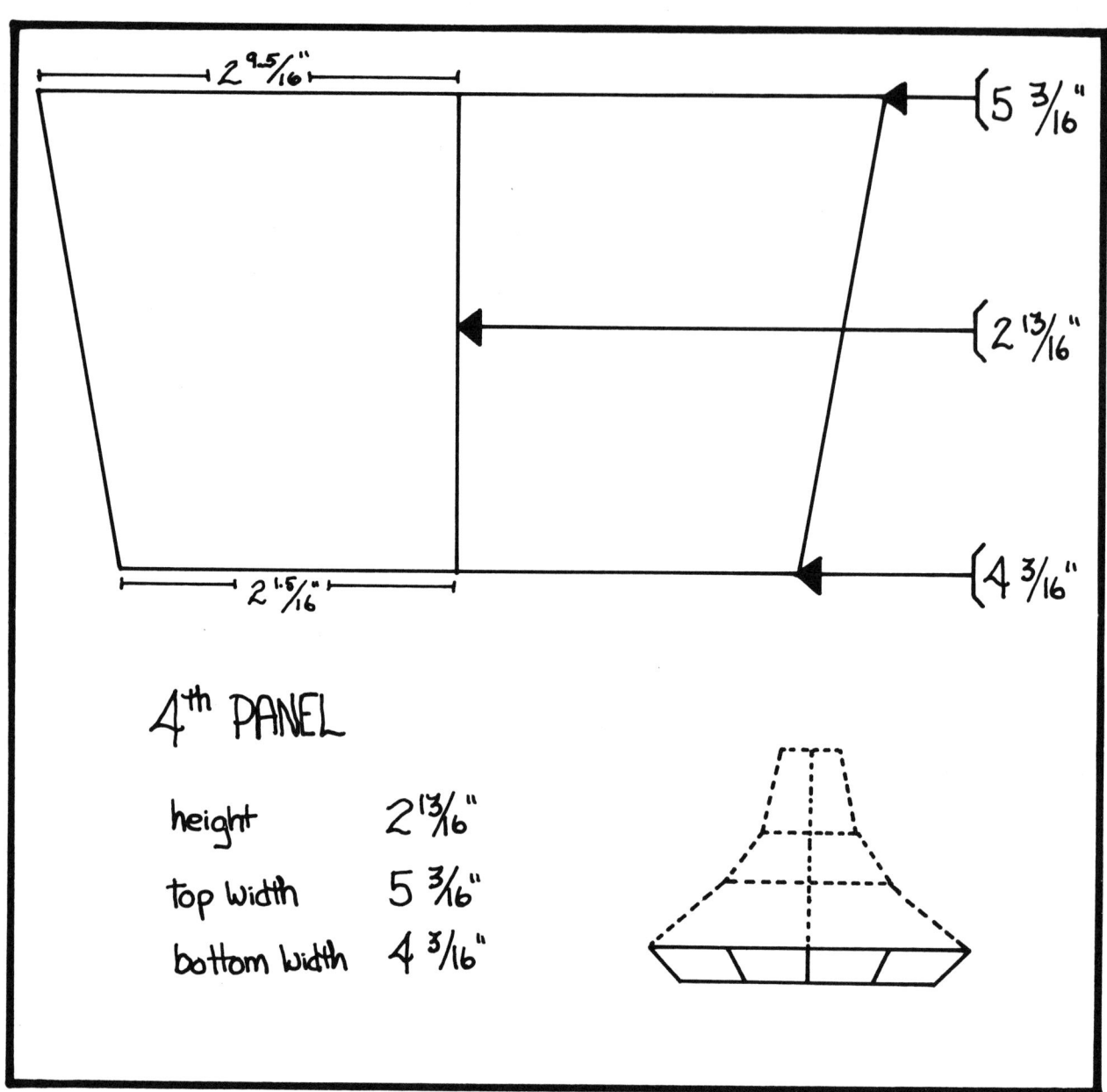

Ill. 10-13

The panels of section 4, the lamp's skirt.

Ill. 10-14

A potpourri of lamps—the small six-paneled design from Chapter 9, a small but intricate twelve-sided creation by Larry Brooks, and two large lamps by the author with four sections of twelve panels each.

BUYING GUIDE

Glass and glassworking supplies are of tantamount importance. You can acquire the correct materials in a few ways. For convenience, check your Yellow Pages for a local supplier or a craft guild that can direct you to one. If you do not find such a company, then use one of the two major mail-order firms listed here. Also, if you are going to use the mail, you might consider getting together with a few friends or a club and ordering bulk materials direct from the manufacturer or major distributor. The following lists cover all of these possibilities.

U.S.A.
Retail Companies

Arizona: Glass Art Studios, Phoenix.

California: Hollander Glass Inc., Long Beach; Nervo Studios, Berkeley; The San Francisco Stained Glass Works, San Francisco.

Massachusetts: Whittemore-Durgin Glass Co., Hanover.

Minnesota: Glass House Studio, St. Paul and Minneapolis.

New Jersey: The Stained Glass Club, Norwood.

New York: The New Rainbow Studio, White Plains; S.A. Bendheim Co., Inc., Manhattan; Glass Masters Guild, Manhattan.
Special N.Y.C. suppliers: City Chemical Corp, Manhattan, for sulfuric acid, glycerine (to make flux), and cupric acid (a dangerous chemical that antiques the finished lead surface); New Era Hardware and Supply, Manhattan, carries Hexacon soldering irons; Conklyn Copper & Brass, Brooklyn, for all raw-metal supplies, copper rods, different weights of sheet copperfoil, thin strips of copper, brass sheet metal, etc.; Teddy's Lamp and Lighting, Manhattan, carries all lamp components in all sizes, including different styles of chains, vase caps, sockets, zip cords, etc.

Pennsylvania: Glenside Glass Co., Glenside, Doylestown, and Quakertown.

Utah: Artistic Glass, Salt Lake City.

Texas: Glass House Studio, Houston.

Small-Quantity

Whittemore-Durgin Glass Co., Box 2065, Hanover, Mass. 02339. Distributors of domestic rolled and antique glass, commercial sheet glass, and imported antique glass, plus an unusual assortment of glass-related objects and fixtures. Send for their free catalog and get on their mailing list.

Nervo Studios, 2027 7th Street, Berkeley, Calif. 94710. Nervo has a large, efficient mail-order business comparable to Whittemore-Durgin. Send $1.00 for their catalog.

Bulk Mail-Order Suppliers

To order glass by the full or small (half) crate, write to the following companies for their price lists:
S.A. Bendheim Co., Inc., 122 Hudson St., N.Y.C., N.Y. 10013.

Kokomo Opalescent Glass Co., Inc., Box 809, Kokomo, Ind. 46901.

Blenko Glass Co. Inc., Milton, West Virginia 25541.

These companies will not ship less than a crate of glass. A full wooden crate containing 20–24 sheets of glass weighs 550–820 pounds. Each full sheet measures approximately 32 inches x 84 inches and weighs approximately 24–30 pounds. The crate itself (with packing material only) weighs 80–100 pounds. A small (or half) wooden crate containing 20–24 half sheets of glass will weight 360–410 pounds. Each half sheet measures approximately 32 inches x 42 inches and weighs approximately 13–15 pounds. The crate (with packing material only) weighs 30–50 pounds.

To order solder in 100–500-pound quantities, write to the following companies for their price lists: White Metal Rolling and Stamping Corp., 80 Moultrie St., Brooklyn, New York 11222; Gardiner Metal Co., 4820 So. Campbell Ave., Chicago, Ill. 60632.
Two other companies do not sell direct to the public, but they will furnish you with the name of a distributor in your town or city, and they will send you a catalog upon request:

Fletcher-Terry Co., Spring Lane, Farmington, Conn. 06032 (tools and special glass-cutting equipment).

Hexacon Electric Co., 161 West Clay Ave., Roselle Park, New Jersey 07204 (soldering irons, rheostats, iron holders, special soldering tips—the recommended soldering iron is listed as Hexacon Plug Tip No. P100, 100 watts, 110–120 volts; it holds a ⅜-inch soldering tip).

Ordering in bulk quantities will save you literally hundreds of dollars. If you have a resale number or if your church or local craft studio has one, you can place wholesale orders with the above companies and save additional money.

Shipping Information

Each supplier has a specific method for handling bulk mail-order sales. However, there are some similarities in procedure.

Purchasing Terms

The following terms are used by large suppliers (cash and C.O.D. are generally not accepted):
1. Established credit terms;
2. Check or money order, prepaid with the purchase order.

Orders are shipped F.O.B.; you are responsible for the shipping or trucking charges. (Shipping costs run from 4 percent to 10 percent of the total value of the shipment.) The purchasing invoice for glass will include: the cost of the glass, a boxing/crating charge, a shipping charge (computed by weight of glass and box/crate), and a state tax. Shipping costs run high, but if the materials are being shipped out of state, you do not pay a state tax on your order. Large shipments will only be delivered to a complete address, not a post-office box.

Claims

If a crate is damaged in shipment, leave it as is and immediately notify the trucking company. Once an authorized person has inspected the damage, it must be noted on all copies of the delivery receipts and a claim filed for reimbursement (usually filed with the trucking company). A similar procedure is followed when the United Parcel Service or Parcel Post delivers a damaged shipment of tools, materials, or small orders of glass.

U.K.

Glass

James Hetley Ltd
10-12 Beresford Avenue
Wembley
Middlesex
(Tel: London 903-4151)

Hartley Wood and Co.
Portobello Glass Works
Portobello Lane
Monkweirmouth
Sunderland
Co. Durham
(Tel: Sunderland 72506)

Hetleys serve the London area, Hartley Wood the rest of the country. Most sorts of glass are available, especially antique, and Hetleys hope to stock copperfoil in the near future.

Other items will have to be found through yellow pages. Solder, soldering iron and glass cutters can be obtained from a do-it-yourself shop; copperfoil, copper rods and brass sheet metal suppliers are listed under "non-ferrous metals"; chemicals such as sulfuric and cupric acid should be available from chemical suppliers.